SMOKE-JUMPER
JUMPER
& OTHER STORIES

ISBN: 978-1-59152-286-7

For more information or to order extra copies of this book
call Farcountry Press toll free at (800) 821-3874.

sweetgrassbooks
an imprint of Farcountry Press

Produced by Sweetgrass Books
PO Box 5630, Helena, MT 59604; (800) 821-3874;
www.sweetgrassbooks.com

Book design by Jess LaGreca

The views expressed by the author/publisher in this book do not necessarily
represent the views of, nor should be attributed to, Sweetgrass Books.
Sweetgrass Books is not responsible for the content of the author/publisher's
work.

Produced and printed in the United States of America.

28 27 26 25 24   3 4 5 6 7

SMOKE-

JUMPER

& OTHER STORIES

"Swede" Troedsson

"Swede" Troedsson

CONTENTS

Author's Preface   ix

Chapter 1 First Season with The U.S. Forest Service   1

Chapter 2 U.S Marine Corps Experiences   5
    Outpost Duty   5
    Rats   6
    Torpedoes   7
    Air Mattress   8

Chapter 3 A Season on the Skykomish Ranger District   11
    Avalanches   11
    Toasted Pickup   12

Chapter 4 Smokejumper Experiences   15
    Kooskia Days   15
    First Fire Jump   16
    Poison Oak   17
    Wading the St. Joe   18
    Fawn Ridge Fire   19
    Warm Springs Creek Fire   20
    Silk Sheets   21
    Hebgen Lake Earthquake Rescue   22
    Chute Malfunction   24
    After Thoughts   24

Chapter 5 N.P.R.R. Forester   27
    Cigars   27
    Wind Shear   28
    Frozen Malones   29
    Busted Nose   29
    Cruise Mark   30

Chapter 6 Forest Service Experiences   31
    Toasted Hardhat   31
    Sarsaparilla Bottle   32
    Ants   33
    Chain Hoist   34
    Bear Spray   34

Slapped Down   35
Watermelon   36
A Good Crew   36
Gatorade   38
Flicker Vertigo   39
Zero 2 Tango   39
Dodging Cranes   40
Pictographs   41
Llamas   42
Mooned   42
Heavy Load   43
Oreo Cookies   44
Sky Cranes   45
Elk Wrestling   46
Flies   48
TFR   48
Fortune Cookie   49
Chapter 7 Canoeing with Wardens   51
Mice   53
Elk Skeleton   60
Chapter 8 Hunting   61
Goat Hunt   61
Elk Retrieval   62
Frozen Elk   64
Choices   64
Duck Hunt   65
Persia   66
Chapter 9 Rescue   69
Saving Hank   69
White Puppy Dog   70
Trapper in Trouble   72
Saving Ken   72
Primate Pills   74
Payback   76
Edmonton   77
Odontoid Process   79
Hang Gliders   80

River Rescue   81

Failure to Yield   82

Perfect Timing   83

Chapter 10 Dogs   85

Harry   85

Urp   85

Trixie   87

Chapter 11 Cats   89

Cat's Ass   89

Bimbo   90

Chapter 12 Other Stories   91

Grapefruit   91

Nine-Toe Jimmy   92

Death Wish   92

Zingers   93

Wallet   94

Coffee   96

.45-110   96

World Record   97

Connection   97

About the Author   101

AUTHOR'S PREFACE

WHAT FOLLOWS ARE stories of my true-life experiences following my high school days. They were submitted to the local *Dillonite Daily*, which published them on a weekly basis.

Many folks who have read these stories have suggested that I publish them in book form.

Credibility of the stories was established by having the drafts reviewed by those involved who still survive and can be contacted. Their contributions are included.

Acknowledgments

A special thanks to Charlene Loge who edited my manuscript and offered improvement suggestions.

The following reviewed and/or contributed to my stories:

- Former Smokejumpers: Carl Gidlund, Lee Lipscomb, Bob Nicol, Roger Savage, Duane Ferdinand, Doug Gordon, Robert Cushing, Stan Bolle, Vance Warren, and Jim Cherry.
- Montana Game Wardens: retired Game Wardens Jim DeBoer and Mike Mehn, and Warden Kerry Wahl.
- Retired Forest Service Officers: Dan Pence, Ron Schott, Frank Fowler, Vergil Lindsey, and Pete Bengeyfield (who provided the elk drive netting photo).
- Former Beaverhead County Sheriff Rick Later, former Dillon Mayor Marty Malesich, Kathy DeRuwe, Adrian Stokes, Jeremia Nygren (Nels Nygren's grandson), Tracey Roberts (Nels Nygren's daughter), Shelly Hartz's letters, Kathy Martinez & Linda Cervelli, Debra Goslin (Trixie's temporary care giver), Jimmy Harrison, Dr. Ron Loge, Brian Mutch, Mary Lou Rowher's records, and genealogist Marian Spenser, and LDS Bishop Kirk Van Slyke, DPT.

Sources of Information

- U. S. Forest Service Rescue case folders: Hank Williams, Jr., and Shelly Hartz.
- Newspaper articles: Dillon *Tribune* (Hank's Rescue and Saving Ken).
- National Smokejumper Association Website Links: Jump List, Smokejumper Records, and R1-R3 Smokejumpers Fire History

Great effort was made not to embellish the stories.

Chapter One

FIRST SEASON WITH THE U.S. FOREST SERVICE

IN JUNE 1953, I was hired as a Fire Lookout by the Superior Ranger District, on the Lolo National Forest, in Montana. I had hitchhiked up from Baton Rouge, Louisiana, where I was attending college at LSU.

After attending a week of "Guard School" at the Nine Mile Remount Depot, I was installed on the Marble Mountain Lookout on the Superior District. The lookout was a 15-square-foot cabin mounted on four 35-foot-long wooden legs. Windows were on all sides. In the off-season, hinged shutters would be lowered over them. When the lookout was occupied, the shutters were propped up. It contained an "alidade" fire locator, two folding metal cots, a table, a chair, a stool, some cabinets, eating and cooking utensils, and a small wood cook stove that included an oven. The basic dry staples were in a "30-day, one man" box. The dry staples were supplemented by fresh vegetables, meat, and other supplies. There was no refrigeration, so, when received, the most perishable food was eaten first, then back to the canned goods. Included in the box was a wonderful Lookout Cookbook. The lookout was far from a water source, so the packer visited twice a month with his mule string packing water in 10-gallon milk cans and fresh food supplies. The water was poured into a 160-gallon buried holding tank.

With the supplies in the box, I could bake six different pies (apple, cherry, raisin, blackberry, blueberry, and peach). The packer, Tom Vann, would call me prior to departing the town of Superior for my lookout and tell me what kind of pie he wanted with coffee when he arrived.

In the evenings I would visit with other lookouts on the telephone. The lookout was situated south of the Clark Fork River, across from the Keystone Game Preserve. At night I could see the lights of the towns of Superior to the east and St. Regis to the west.

Shortly after arriving at the lookout, I looked for a broom. The broom I found was in shambles. I called the District and requested they send a replacement broom. They informed me that they had forgotten to replace the broom. The previous summer the lookout was "manned" by two elderly sisters. They had been tossing food down to a black bear, who routinely returned for handouts. One evening, shortly after retiring to bed, they felt the tower shaking. It was the black bear climbing up the tower stairs looking for a handout. One of the sisters charged out in her nightgown with the broom and beat on the bear and chased it off. And this is how the broom was demolished.

There was a garbage pit, covered with logs and soil, located a short way downslope from the lookout. Access to the pit was through a one-foot-square hole with a removable lid.

One evening, from my catwalk, I witnessed a black bear trying to get into my garbage pit. He had removed the lid but could not get his shoulders through the hole. He turned around, plunked his butt into the hole, and was wiggling it in order to widen the hole. He ran off when he heard me laughing.

The packer brought up a can of creosote on his next trip. After spreading creosote over the top of the pit, I had no further bear problems.

The lookout was grounded against lightning. The feet of the stool legs were inserted in glass power line insulators. We were instructed that during severe lightning storms we should sit on the stool.

One evening, while lying on my cot, a severe lightning storm sent electrical arcs shooting from the stove to the alidade. One tremendous lightning strike sent an electrical arc from the stove to the alidade, then from the alidade to my cot, giving me quite a start!

There was a salt lick behind my lookout. A large bull elk would routinely arrive to lick on it.

On one of his trips, I asked Tom why he carried a holstered Colt .45 caliber revolver, hanging off his saddle horn. He told me that the previous summer he had been packing supplies in to a trail crew, including a replacement chainsaw. While crossing a bridge across a draw, a mule broke through the bridge and fell into the draw. The mule had one leg stuck in the mud, which appeared broken. Tom was trying to figure out how to put the mule out of its misery. He had no pistol then. His gaze fell on the chainsaw. He crawled down into the draw with the chainsaw, and after starting it, began to approach the mule, who was desperately trying to pull its leg out of the mud. Tom said that the closer he got to the mule, the bigger the mule's eyes got. He was about to sink the saw into the mule's neck when it gave a final desperate lunge and pulled its leg out of the mud. The mule was fine.

If Tom would have had a pistol that day, he might have killed a good mule. But he swore he would never again be without a pistol while traveling with his string of mules.

After six weeks on the lookout, I spent the rest of the summer helping clear trails and piling logging slash. We lived in a trailer while on the slash piling project area. One evening a young black bear raided our food cache, which we kept stored in a cooler in a creek bottom. We clipped onto a Forest Service telephone line and notified the district. The Assistant Ranger came up and shot the bear. We cooked and ate a nice bear roast.

After terminating my summer employment, I hitchhiked to Minneapolis to visit an uncle and his family. On the way, I spent one night on an Iowa pig farmer's couch. After visiting my uncle, I hitch hiked back east to visit my Dad, before returning to college.

It was a great summer!

Chapter Two

U.S. MARINE CORPS EXPERIENCES

Outpost Duty

IN THE SPRING of 1954, I was flunking out of college. Ashamed of wasting my Dad's money, I decided to join the Marines. This would earn me the G.I. Bill and give me time to determine if I really wanted a college education. If I decided to go for it, the G.I. Bill would help me finance it.

I signed up for the two-year Active Reserve program and went through "Boot" Camp in San Diego. I was interviewed about my job experience. I explained that I had worked the previous summer as a Fire Lookout. The interviewer wanted to know what that was about. I explained that I was stationed in a 35-foot tower looking for fires. If I spotted one, I was to determine the location and call it in.

At the conclusion of my bootcamp training, I, along with men in my platoon, were assigned Specialty Numbers. Most of the men in my platoon were assigned 0300 (Basic Infantry). A few lucky ones were assigned to Air Wing. I was the only one assigned an 0200. Thinking it might be a "typo," I went to my Drill Instructor (D.I.) and inquired as to what 0200 meant. He said he would make a telephone call. I overheard him exclaim: "What? That dummy!"

Following the phone inquiry, my D.I. returned and said: "Private. I don't know how YOU got it, but that's Intelligence."

Being Swedish, I had to ask, "What's Intelligence?" He said he didn't exactly know, but he understood the "Kill Ratio" was quite high in those guys.

Following Boot Camp, I was given leave to return home for a brief visit. Upon returning from leave, I received combat training at Camp Pendleton. Then I was shipped to Korea in the summer of 1954. This was after the Truce had been signed. I was assigned to the 1st Marine Division. My assignment was to help man outposts on the DMZ (38th Parallel). I, along with other men, would do rotating 30-day hitches manning 20-foot towers. During daylight hours we would spot North Koreans, "shoot" azimuths on them, and call them in. Nighttime duty was to serve as an early warning system should the North Koreans decide to "jump the line." One day an officer told me: "Private, you're the only Marine in the history of the Corps to be assigned to what he did in civilian life." We lived in tents and bunkers, not a comfortable situation in the winter of 1954-55.

The nicest part of my tour in Korea was a week of R&R (Rest & Recuperation) in Kyoto, Japan. The saddest part was having to put my dog down.

I adopted a stray dog and trained it to sleep on the foot of my cot. This would keep the rats off of me. I fed the dog scraps from the mess hall, and less desirable contents from C-rations. One day I was ordered to put the dog down because it had developed mange. I tried to recruit others to do it but was turned down. I finally had to do it through tear-filled eyes.

In the spring of 1955, we were relieved by the Army. We loaded up on ships and sailed back to the U.S.A. On the way, we crossed the International Date Line on St. Patrick's Day. This resulted in two St. Patrick's Day in a row. By coincidence, my first child would be born on St. Patrick's Day.

Following the completion of my active duty, I went on to finish my college education. My dad paid for the tuition and books. Summer employments as a "timber beast" and as a Smokejumper, along with the GI Bill, paid for all other costs. Time in the Marines was time well spent. I became proficient at shooting a rifle and operating a mop. The real benefit was I developed a desire to finish college and had earned the G.I. Bill.

Rats

During 1954-1955 I was stationed in Korea with the First Marine Division. Part of my duties was manning outposts along the DMZ (38th parallel). We pulled rotating 30-day shifts, living in bunkers and tents, and serving as an early detection system should the North Koreans decide to "jump the line."

The area was heavily populated with rats. Lots of rats. BIG RATS! (Dan Pence, who served with the Army in Korea, recalls the rats being "as big as cats.")

With the numerous rice paddies and decomposing bodies, they had a plentiful food base.

Some of these rats carried fleas, which could transmit a hemorrhagic fever virus. This virus would damage the walls of tiny blood vessels. In fatal cases, the victim would internally hemorrhage to death. The sclera (whites of the eyes) would turn flaming red just prior to death. Capt. Black, our Company Commanding Officer (C.O.), survived this infection.

At night, prior to turning out the light, leftovers from food packages from home would be stored in .50 cal. ammo cans so rats would not demolish the food.

One of the men in our bunker was a "White Russian" named Issador Riggalo. One night I awoke to Issador shouting and cursing. When I shined my flashlight on Issador, he was sitting upright on his cot. Blood was trickling down the bridge of his nose.

Issador explained that he awoke to something warm lying on his forehead. When he reached up to grab it, a rat bit him.

Another night, in our bunker, I awoke to a snuffling and scrabbling noise next to my cot. I shined my flashlight on the source of the noise. The noise came from a large rat caught by its nose in a rat trap. I pounded it to death with the butt end of my M-1 rifle.

One night I was returning to my company area from a patrol. On my way back to my tent, I passed by the communications bunker, which was manned 24/7. Lantern light shown through the entrance. I heard pistol shots from inside the bunker. When I peeked into the bunker, I could see the shadow of a large rat running across one of the bunker beams. The duty radioman, out of pure boredom, would track the rat with his .45 pistol, shoot, and usually miss. Sand would trickle out of the bullet hole in the sandbag.

Oh, well, at least the rats were providing entertainment for a bored radioman!

Torpedoes

During 1954–1956 I served with the First Marine Division in Korea. A good buddy of mine, Silvio Sante Solare (I'll never forget that name) would receive food packages from home. (Silvio's family owned a winery in Napa, California). The packages would quite often contain spaghetti and the makings for spaghetti sauce.

We would obtain hamburger and tomato sauce from a buddy who worked as a cook in the mess hall kitchen and make a huge spaghetti feast. Among those invited was the cook, and a medical corpsman who would bring 200 proof medicinal alcohol.

We would mix the alcohol with grapefruit juice. We called the drink torpedoes. We'd pig out on spaghetti and get sloshed on torpedoes!

After our division returned to Camp Pendleton, California, Silvio took me to his home in Napa on a weekend liberty. We visited his family's wine-tasting room and had a great weekend.

In 2001 I was visiting some first cousins in California. During my visit they took me on a tour of the wineries in Napa. During the course of our tour, I happened to mention my Marine Corps buddy Silvio Solare, and that his family owned a winery in Napa. My cousins stated that the Solare winery was close by, so we stopped in to visit.

I approached the receptionist at the visitor center and explained that I had served with Silvio in Korea. The receptionist stated that Silvio was her Uncle, and was living in Albuquerque, New Mexico. She gave me his telephone number.

When I arrived back home, I was able to contact Silvio. We had a great visit. Unfortunately, Silvio was suffering from prostate cancer. This is the last I heard from him. I suspect the cancer finally took him.

Air Mattress

In the spring of 1955, I returned from Korea. The rest of my active duty commitment with the Marine Corps was spent that year at Camp Pendleton, California.

One day, several of us drove to Oceanside to enjoy swimming, and to flirt with the "eye candy" in their bikinis. I took along a government air mattress for floating on the ocean.

We returned to the base well after dark. The Military Policemen (MPs) were inspecting vehicles entering the base for contraband. While inspecting the trunk of our car, a HUGE MP discovered the air mattress. Upon inquiring who belonged to the mattress, I admitted it was me. The MP accused me of illegal use of government property and said he would take me to the brig. He instructed me to get into the back of his pickup truck with the air mattress and wait there while he inspected some more arriving vehicles.

I threw the air mattress into our car trunk and told my buddies to head for our barracks.

The MP returned to take me to the Oceanside brig. He asked me if I had the air mattress in the truck with me. I replied: "Sure do."

Upon arriving at the brig, the MP instructed me to follow him into the brig. The brig Duty Sergeant asked: "Now, what has this Marine done?" The MP explained the misuse of the government air mattress. The Sergeant asked: "Where's the mattress?" The MP turned to me and asked: "Where's the mattress?"

I replied: "What mattress?"

The Sergeant blew up and chewed out the MP for bringing me in without the evidence. He then instructed the MP to drive me to my barracks.

It was a very quiet trip back to the base. I was plastered next to the passenger door hoping this huge pissed-off MP would not pound this skinny 140-pound Marine into salt.

When we got to within a mile of my barracks, the MP said this was close enough and to walk the rest of the way. Relieved to leave the MP, I walked the remaining mile.

Upon arriving at the barracks, I approached the duty desk and asked the night duty marine to connect me with the Oceanside brig. I informed the brig Duty Sergeant that the MP had disobeyed his orders and made me walk the remaining mile to my barracks.

Fifteen minutes later I was told to return to the phone. A VERY angry MP advised me to NEVER come through his gate again when he was on duty. I never saw that MP again!

Cruise Camp on Maloney Mountain. *Left to right:* "Swede"
Johnson, "Swede" Troedsson, Jack Reynolds
Photo courtesy Bob Norton

Chapter Three

A SEASON ON THE SKYKOMISH RANGER DISTRICT

Avalanches

IN THE SUMMER of 1957, I was stationed as a summer temporary timber aide on the Skykomish Ranger District on the Snoqualmie National Forest in northwest Washington.

The district butts up against the top of the Cascade Mountain Range. In the winter snow depths on parts of the district approach 40 feet. The district is just west of the Stevens Pass Ski Area.

The district is BIG avalanche country. On March 1, 1910, an avalanche swept two trains, trapped by snowdrifts just west of Stevens Pass, off the tracks. 96 people lost their lives. It remains the worst avalanche disaster in the history of the United States. (The story can be found by searching 1910 Stevens Pass Avalanche Disaster on the Internet.)

In June, Timber Technician Bob Norton and I were tasked with measuring the dimensions of a huge avalanche debris area. An avalanche had roared down a draw the previous winter and deposited a large tangle of huge Douglas Fir and Spruce trees. The objective was to determine the acreage of the debris area, and by applying average per acre volume in adjacent standing timber, determine the volume of salvageable timber in the debris area. Once the salvageable timber volume was determined, after applying a generous "cull & breakage" estimate, the district would advertise the timber for salvage.

Bob and I were measuring the cross dimension of the debris area when his dog, Smokey, started barking at something in the debris. There was still snow packed in the bottom of the debris. We could hear a creek gurgling at the bottom of this tangle of trees.

Bob went over to Smokey to see what was getting the dog so excited. When Bob got to the dog, he called me over to see what the dog had found. Sticking out of the debris was a black bear's head, still well preserved in the cool environment. That's all we could find. We suspect the bear was denned up when the avalanche roared down, tearing the head off the bear.

Later, I was sharing this story with a local tree faller. He told me he had found a dead mountain goat on a timber sale he had been working on. It appeared to him the goat had been killed by an avalanche.

Toasted Pickup

We had just completed laying out a 52-million-board-foot timber sale on Maloney Mountain when a fire broke out on state and private land below the timber sale. I drove up to the Maloney Mountain Lookout, situated above the fire, to join District Ranger John Sarginson, who was already there sizing up the fire. He pointed to a Forest Service pickup towing a water trailer that was approaching the fire and asked me to run down to the pickup and drive it up to the lookout so he could retrieve his caulked boots (boots with spiked soles).

When I arrived at the pickup, it was parked just below a steep switchback. I realized that the two-wheel-drive pickup, pulling a water trailer, could not make it up and around the steep switchback (later determined to be an 18-percent grade).

A logger in a four-wheel-drive pickup offered to attach a tow chain to the pickup, and tow me up and around the switchback. By then hot smoke was boiling over the switchback.

After attaching a tow chain to the pickup, the logger proceeded to tow me up and around the switchback. Two seasonal employees were riding in the bed of the pickup. By then hot embers were falling on the pickup. In the middle of it all, the tow chain came undone from the front of my truck. The logger's pickup just kept going up through the smoke. I was stuck, I couldn't go forward, and I couldn't back up with the attached trailer. The two men riding in the back of the pickup jumped in the cab with me to escape the falling embers. I told them to jump out and run up the road and out of the hot smoke. Shortly thereafter, I grabbed the ranger's boots and bailed out of the truck. I ran uphill through the hot smoke and falling embers and walked up to the lookout.

The pickup gas tank had been topped off with gasoline that morning. The gasoline got to boiling, the filler cap popped off, and the gasoline poured onto the ground and ignited. The truck, including a nice compass in the glove box and the trailer, were completely consumed by the fire.

1958, First Training Jump

Chapter Four

SMOKEJUMPER EXPERIENCES

Kooskia Days

ON JULY 3, 1958, I cracked my left fibula on my second training jump. After getting fitted with a lower leg cast and crutches, I was sent to the Clearwater National Forest Supervisor's Office in Orofino, Idaho. It was there I was assigned the mundane task of auditing timber survey sheets.

In late July an office clerk suggested I drive down to Kooskia, Idaho, to attend their annual celebration, which occurs over the last weekend in July. (Kooskia is on the east edge of the Nez Perce Indian Reservation.)

On that Saturday I drove down to the jump base in Grangeville and alerted the jumpers about the celebration in Kooskia. I returned to Kooskia with Sam Rost (GAC-58)*, Doug Getz (GAC-58), and one other jumper whose name I forget, in tow.

Upon arriving in Kooskia we walked into a bar. The place was packed with people celebrating wildly. We stood in the middle of the floor with can of beer in hand, watching the celebration. Across from us, against a wall, was a table where three good looking women sat. The table was covered with free drinks.

After a short while, I noticed a very attractive Indian woman sitting at the

---

*(GAC-'58) means this jumper was initially trained at the Grangeville Air Center in 1958. (MSO-'59) means this jumper was initially trained at Missoula in 1959.

bar. Noticing no wedding band, I clumped over to the bar on my crutches with the intent of pitching a little woo.

Things were going great until the woman informed me that the only other man who had kissed her like that was her husband. I hastily clumped back to rejoin my "bros."

So, there we were, "innocent children" from Montana taking all of this in. Eventually, a fellow who I guessed was in his early twenties intentionally kicked a crutch out from under me as he passed by on his way to the end of the room to join some of his buddies. He stood there pointing at me as he and his buddies were laughing at me. I was doing a slow torch.

I stopped this fellow on his way out and reminded him that he kicked my crutch out from under me. He stuck his chin out and said: "Oh yeah, so what are going to do about it?" There was a month of frustration behind my punch. He back pedaled and crashed into that table load of women. Drinks spilled, women screamed, and when he clawed his way back up, I hit him again. Three loggers came to my aid, grabbed the guy up, and threw him out onto the street.

After six weeks I shed my cast. I was assigned to a timber survey crew and spent the rest of the summer on the Clearwater National Forest. It turned out to be a pretty good summer.

First Fire Jump

On July 10, 1959, we completed the last of our seven training jumps. This followed a month of intense phyical conditioning, and training in the skills we would need as Smokejumpers.

Two weeks later, I and 16 others "boosted" to Redding, California, in a DC-3 (aka "Gooney Bird") to assist in a rash of fires. On final approach to the Redding Airport, Duane Ferdinand (MSO-59), a ranch boy from Lewistown, Montana, mentioned, with a big grin, that this was his eighth flight on a plane and the first time to have landed in one.

On July 25, 1959, under the leadership of foreman Al Cramer (MSO-43), all seventeen of us were dispatched to the Ramshorn Creek Fire. The fire was located in the Trinity Alps, on the Shasta–Trinity National Forest. Besides me, there were six others in the crew who had never jumped on a fire. As we suited up the temperature was a scorching 108 degrees.

Carl Gidlund (MSO-58) recalls that the fire was in a well-roaded area not too far from Redding. But, because it was boiling, jumpers were called to get men on the ground as soon as possible.

Carl also recalls: "—it was an extremely bumpy flight, and we circled the fire many times. My recollection is that the jumper seated next to the cockpit got sick. No burp bags were available in those days, so he vomited into a seamless sack then passed it, dripping, to the door to be tossed out. As the bag was passed from hand to hand, several of those who got a whiff of it also threw up. I wasn't the guilty party, but I was beginning to feel the urge too, so I dashed to the door and made sure I was one of the first sticks to exit."

We finally started jumping. The jump spot was a fenced field surrounded by trees. Again, Carl recalls: "A high voltage transmission line bisected the jump spot. Jumper Eddy Noel (MSO-59) was blown into it and his parachute was draped over a pair of lines, causing an arc. A few of us on the ground counseled Eddy to release his capewells simultaneously. If he released only a single one and his body hit the ground while the chute was still tangled in the line, he would have completed the circuit and probably would have been electrocuted. He did release both and fell safely to the ground."

When it was my turn to jump, Duane Ferdinand and I jumped in the same stick. As we descended, we shouted to one another in an effort to avoid colliding with each other. Much to my surprise, several horses ran out from under the tree shade. They appeared to be in a panic, running back and forth. I assumed it was because they could hear voices but could not see where they came from. I was so concerned about possibly colliding with a horse or having one tangle in my chute that I made a sloppy landing. I took the brunt of the landing-shock on my wallet which was located in my left hip pocket. I lay there thinking I'd broken my hip. Duane heard my groaning and ran over to check on me and helped me to my feet.

We all were trucked up to the fire line, but by two o'clock in the morning my "glute" had stiffened so badly that I had to go to camp. By this time the fire was 3,000 acres.

The next day we were released from the fire and returned to Redding. We later heard that by the second night the fire had grown to over 10,000 acres, after having burned through camp.

Poison Oak

On July 18, 1959, thirteen of us led by Al Cramer (MSO-43) were dispatched to the Water Gulch Fire. The fire was located on the shore of Lake Shasta.

Upon arrival, we observed that there was a line around the fire. A barge, with a dozer on board, was headed our way. While circling around the fire and over the lake, recreational motorboats were circling underneath us to watch the jump show.

My jump partner and I were kicked out early and landed on the lake shore, close to the water. A motorboat roared up to us. The operator offered to take us to join the rest of our crew. We gladly accepted!

The rest of the jumpers landed in a tall brush field. They were commenting on the fact that the brush had provided such a cushy landing.

It turned out the fire was already contained, so all we did was gather our gear and return to Redding.

Little did we realize that the brush was poison oak. As I recall, six of our crew were off the jump list for two weeks, recuperating from a poison oak inflammation.

Lee Lipscomb (MSO-58) recalls, "Anyway I remember very well the poison oak problem as I pulled my parachute off the heavy growth of it and then stuffed it into my paper sleeping bag for warmth. Well this meant I got the worst case of poison oak of my entire life and was hospitalized for one or two days when we got back to Redding. I recall we were removed from the fire by a garbage barge which came to pick us up."

Wading the St. Joe

On August 1, 1959, Jerrold (Jerry) Daniels (MSO-58) and I were dispatched from Missoula in a Twin Beech to the Bacon Creek Fire. The spot fire was on the south side of the St. Joe River, on the Red Ives Ranger District, in the St. Joe National Forest, Idaho. The spotter was Harry Roberts (MSO-53).

Upon starting to exit the aircraft, the prop blast momentarily pinned me against the small door frame. Harry gave me a STRONG shove, which propelled me out the door. After a non-eventful parachute landing, we had the fire out by late that afternoon. The next morning, we packed up our gear, and proceeded to make the pack out north from the Bacon Peak ridge down to the St. Joe River. The pack out to the river was a rough cross-country one-and-a-half miles and took almost two hours.

We had to wade the river in order to get to the St. Joe River trail on the north side of the river. The trail would lead us to the Red Ives Ranger Station.

The water was up to our knees. Here I was, a 140-pound pin butt, with a 100-pound pack, on slippery rocks, trying desperately to avoid doing a face plant in the river. My lack of good traction was compounded by boots with smooth neoprene soles.

We made it across without incident. After stacking our gear on the trail, (to be picked up later by a packer), we walked about ten miles down-river to the ranger station.

After getting cleaned up, we were driven to Avery that evening, where we had dinner. We later boarded the late-night Milwaukee train to Missoula, arriving in the early morning.

Fawn Ridge Fire

On August 3, 1959, eight of us, under leadership of Bob Nicol (MSO-52) were dispatched from Missoula to the Fawn Ridge Fire, located in the Salmon River drainage, on the Bitterroot National Forest. The spotter was Roland "Andy" Andersen (MSO-52), and the Assistant Spotter was Larry Nelsen (MSO-56). Bob Nicol's jump log shows that Cookie Calloway was the pilot in the DC-2, N4867V.

The jump spot was on a ridge with huge ponderosa pine trees. Roger Savage (MSO-57) states that the Master Action Sheets show the following: The fire was jumped at 1800; was reached at 1830; was controlled by 2100; and we left the fire at 1440 the next day.

Bob Nicol further recalls, "we had the fire pretty much out that evening and started mopping up. The next morning, we completed the mop up and stacked our gear next to the trail. About noon we declared it out and hiked down to Lantz Bar."

Bob further states: "Frank Lantz was an older prospector who filed a mining claim where Little Squaw creek runs into the main Salmon River. That was probably in the late 1920s or 1930s. He was a very interesting person and I had heard about him from my father who worked on the Magruder district in the mid 1930s. I don't think he ever had a homestead deed for the property."

Bob further relates from his jump log: "Anyway, as we were not issued a radio, we had not had contact with anyone since the jump and I figured that he [Frank] would be on the backcountry telephone line. And he was. One of the first things he told me was that 'Your boat will be here in an hour or so.' Needless to say, I was pleasantly surprised and so was the crew. I had heard about the new jet boats that were working the Salmon River but had never seen one." Bob Cushing (MSO-59) recalls—"the jet boat was the only thing powerful enough to get us up the Salmon River." (A boat ride would save us a 12-mile hike to the Corn Creek boat ramp).

While waiting for the jet boat Frank turned us loose in his beautiful orchard and garden.

Bob continues: "When the boat showed up, we piled in and took off upstream. What a deal! Sitting in comfortable chairs, enjoying the ride and the guide even provided us with a big ice chest full of all kinds of nectars."

Bob states further: "In much too short of time we arrived at the Corn Creek boat ramp. That is where the road to the outside world ended and to the best of my knowledge it still ends there. A Forest Service truck took us to the Salmon station where we spent the night. The following morning one of the Johnson Flying Service DC-3s came in and flew us back to Missoula."

Warm Springs Creek Fire

Late in the afternoon of August 8, 1959, fifteen of us Smokejumpers, under the leadership of foreman Leonard (Len) Krout (MSO-46), were dispatched from Missoula in the DC-3 to the Warm Springs Creek Fire on the Salmon National Forest. (Warm Springs Creek flows into the Middle Fork of the Salmon River). The spotter was Don Morrissey (MSO-55), and the assistant spotter was Dick Tracy (MSO-53). We arrived over the fire late in the afternoon. Carl Gidlund (MSO-58) recalls "As we circled the fire, we noted that its point of origin was next to a cabin and it fanned out as it ran uphill."

Jim Cherry (MSO-57) recalls that: "the winds were really squirrely—One minute the smoke was blowing horizontal and another minute it was going straight up. The country was steep."

Roger Savage (MSO-57) states that the Master Action Sheet shows that the fire was jumped at 1930 on the eighth, and we left the fire on the 10th.

With daylight fading fast, "squirrely winds," a fast-moving fire, and extremely steep country, things did not look good. I suspect all sphincters were flexed. One jumper was reluctant to jump, and according to Carl ". . . scooted to the front of the aircraft." After the rest of us jumped, the plane circled a couple of times before the reluctant jumper was convinced to jump.

Carl recalls: "—I landed in rocks." Jim states: "—guys were landing all over the place. Amazingly, I don't recall anyone being hurt on landing."

By the time the plane finished dropping cargo, its position lights winking, "flying light" was almost done. Len signaled the plane with a flashlight that everyone was safe. We donned headlamps and built line all night. Jim recalls: "The country was—somewhat open with lots of bear grass that was tough to chop through to make a fire line." By daybreak we had the fire lined.

Jim also recalls: "We had a couple of pumps dropped to us and were able to pump water from the spring partway up the slope and into a holding basin we made with tarps, and then, with the other pump we were able to move water up even higher to hit the line. Only time I remember being able to use a pump and water on a fire. I'm guessing the pumps came the morning following our jump. They were probably requested when the potential for water use was recognized."

Duane Ferdinand (MSO-59) states "My notes—say that the fire was 80 to 100 acres."

Jim recounted: "I saw Ray Schenck (MSO-56) using two Pulaskis as canes as he backed his way down the mountain. Years of hard use of his knees had taken their toll. Swollen and sore, Ray had to back down. There was no other option; there was no shame in it either."

When we were released from the fire, we walked a couple of miles to the Flying B Ranch airstrip. From there we returned to Missoula in the Ford Tri-motor (aka "Tin Goose").

Silk Sheets

On August 13, 1959, late in the afternoon, Jon Disler (MSO-58) and I were dispatched to the S. Fork Callahan Creek Fire. The lightning caused spot fire was on the Troy Ranger District, west of Libby, in northwest Montana. We flew to the fire in a Twin Beech. The spotter was Ray Schenck (MSO-56).

Upon arriving over the fire, Jon was kicked out first. By the time the Beech came back around to kick me out, Jon had landed and headed to the fire. When I landed, Jon was not there. I shouted to determine his location, but there was no response.

Before I exited the aircraft, Ray never pointed out the fire to me. So here I was, trying to determine if the fire was located up or down the mountain. With darkness not too far away, I didn't want to go hunting for a fire in the dark without a headlamp. Our fire packs, which contained the headlamps, had been parachuted down to us and were nowhere to be seen.

I figured the best thing for me to do was to sit tight and wait for Jon to come get me. When night fell, I rolled up in my chute and slept the night on my landing spot.

Jon recalls that he shouted out to me, and hearing no response, decided to head to the fire.

In the morning Jon came up to get me, and we walked down the mountain to the fire. The fire was in dry soil cover (duff). We lined the fire, and then proceeded to mop it up. There was no moist soil on site in which to mix the embers. We spent most of the day putting hot embers in our hardhats and walking over to an area containing moist soil in which we could mix in the embers.

By that evening we had the fire out. The following morning (the 15th) we left the fire and were transported to the Troy Ranger Station, where we cleaned up and were fed. We spent the night in the ranger station bunkhouse.

The next morning, we were transported to Troy to board a bus to Missoula. When the bus arrived, the bus driver began to load luggage into the luggage bin. Upon spotting our 100-pound packs, the driver pointed to us and said, "YOU load those into the bin." We did. The bus trip to Missoula was uneventful.

Hebgen Lake Earthquake Rescue

Around 11:30 p.m. on August 17, 1959, several of us were returning from our favorite watering hole, called the Swallow Inn, to the Smokejumper dorm in Missoula. We were approaching the dorm when we felt the ground shaking from the earthquake at Hebgen Lake.

About nine o'clock the next morning, twelve of us boarded the Johnson Flying Service DC-2. First aid and rescue gear were also loaded on board. The pilot was Mel "Cookie" Callaway. The jumper in charge was Al Hammond (MSO-46) and the spotters were Randall (Randy) Hurst (MSO-54) and Joe Roemer (MSO-52). We took off about 9:30.

A little after 10:30 a.m. we arrived over the earthquake area. Cookie had to thread our way through sight-seeing aircraft. The normal late morning wind was starting up, and between trying to dodge private aircraft, increasing wind, circling to identify jump spots, throwing out drift streamers to check the wind, and kicking out jumpers and cargo, it was pretty spooky.

Eight of our crew were kicked out in an area between the slide and the Hebgen Lake Dam.

It is my understanding that by the time jumpers landed, the badly injured had already been evacuated to West Yellowstone. The more seriously injured were then transferred to Bozeman.

Bob Nicole (MSO-52) states: "To the best of my memory the jumpers were the first to arrive on the ground at the site. The helicopters did not start showing up for an hour or two later. Hammond and three jumped right in the parking lot on the dam which served as a helicopter landing site."

"The road coming in from WYS (West Yellowstone) was impassable for several hours after we arrived. Andy, myself, and two others landed in the lower site called rescue point. We had to clear some brush and trees before helos could land. Ground vehicles were not able to get there until late afternoon. All the jump crew were driven to the old jump base at WYS arriving about dark. We all returned to Quake Lake the next morning to continue the search and in the late afternoon went back to WYS where we were then flown to MSO in a DC-3."

(A more detailed account of the Smokejumper involvement in this rescue is available online under "Jumper Recounts Yellowstone Quake Rescue" by Bob Nicol.)

Two of us, Vance Warren (MSO-54) and I, were held back in the aircraft because there was a report of injured at Cliff Lake. Upon arriving over Cliff Lake, we were informed by Forest Service personnel on site that there were no injured. A couple had been killed when a boulder rolled through their tent. We then flew to Ennis, landing at the Sportsman Lodge air field.

Vance and I deplaned and were transported to an area below the slide to assist in the off-loading of personnel that had been trapped above the slide and evacuated by helicopter. The pilot of the helicopter was Fred Gerlach, one of my Missoula forestry school professors. (Fred received the National Pilot of the Year Award for his participation in the rescue operation.)

I was amazed at all the clothing, bedding, and tents stuck in the trees, deposited there by the wind blast from the slide. After assisting with the unloading of survivors off the helicopter, we were returned to Ennis.

The command center in Ennis was in the fire hall. A woman was manning the radio next to a big red button, with instructions to press the button to blow the siren should she get word that the dam had broken. Shortly after the quake, due to a faulty report that the dam had failed, the town was evacuated. Residents returned after being assured that the dam still held.

I was really impressed by the quiet efficiency of the Salvation Army. They drove down from Butte to Ennis in a truck full of clothing. Most of the people evacuated to Ennis were still in their pajamas.

A major problem in this rescue operation was lack of good radio communication between Ennis and the slide area. Vance and I accompanied the forest radio technician to the top of the Virginia City Hill in order to set up a repeater. This attempt to establish radio communication with the slide area was unsuccessful.

The second day, a Twin Beech was on final approach to the Sportsman Lodge airfield when the landing gear clipped a power line located just off the south end of the runway.

The power line fell onto the grass, started a fire, and the woman in the fire hall pushed that big red button.

Needless to say, folks in town got pretty excited until they found out what the siren was about.

Vance and I returned to Missoula the next day.

Chute Malfunction

On the morning of August 25, 1959, Henry (Hank) Trimble (MSO-59) and I were dispatched from Missoula in a Twin Beech to the Maud Creek Fire. The spotter was Thomas "TJ" Thompson (MSO-55), and the assistant spotter was Dick Tracy (MSO-53)

The small spot fire was near White Sand Lake, on the Powell Ranger District, currently on the Clearwater National Forest, Idaho.

Hank was kicked out first over a meadow. I followed, and after opening shock, I sensed I was descending faster than normal, and heard a sound like sheets flapping in a strong wind. Upon checking my canopy, I saw that I had a "line over." I had no steering control of my chute and was headed towards a HUGE boulder. I reached for a knife mounted on the top of my reserve chute, with the intent of cutting the line. I no sooner got the top flap of the knife case open, when the line slipped off the top of my canopy. I was able to steer clear of the boulder and make a safe landing.

This area next to the lake is gorgeous. We had the fire out by that evening, and we made camp in the meadow. We slept in the open under a brilliant star-filled sky. During the night, elk walked right through the meadow.

The next morning, after making a final check of the fire, we stacked our gear on a nearby trail. We then hiked fourteen miles to the Colt Creek Cabin. There we were met by a pickup truck and returned to Missoula.

After Thoughts

I wound up the 1988 fire season as an Air Support Supervisor on a fire near Cooke City, Montana. One evening I had dinner in Cooke City with an Evergreen helicopter pilot. I was telling him about managing helicopter pilots. I always tried to get them into a motel, and if they HAD to get to a telephone (this was before cell phones) on the pretense of getting a mechanic or a relief pilot, I tried my best to get them to a telephone. Some of these pilots were on marriage two or working on number three. I suspected they really wanted to talk to their new girlfriend or their attorney. I didn't need their problems distracting them from safely transporting our fire fighters.

The Evergreen pilot said that this was called "AIDS" in their profession. When I ask him what AIDS stood for, he said it stood for Aviation Induced Divorce Syndrome. I told him I knew some former Smokejumpers that had suffered from that same affliction.

Some time ago, I was dating a woman in Red Lodge, Montana. She introduced me to a friend who retired as a commercial airline pilot with a major airline. I am impressed with the number of commercial airline pilots who retire and decide to buy or build a fancy home and live in Red Lodge.

Her friend was hosting a barbeque, and we were invited. As I was sitting there sipping a "G&T" and nibbling on fancy hors d'oeuvres, the host pointed me out to several of his retired commercial airline buddies and said, "That fellow was a Smokejumper." That caught their attention, and one of them inquired as to what type of planes I had jumped out of. I replied: "Ford Tri-motor, DC-2, DC-3, Travel Air, and Twin Beech." They exploded in laughter. I admitted that this no doubt dated me.

In 1959, the following transportation methods were used to return me from Smokejumper fire assignments to Missoula: pickup truck (Lochsa River, Idaho); DC-3 (Redding, California, & Salmon, Idaho); Ford Trimotor (S. Fk Salmon River, Idaho); jet boat (Salmon River, Idaho); train (Avery, Idaho); bus (Troy, Montana); and garbage barge (Lake Shasta, California)!

For those who would like to listen to interviews with current and former Smokejumpers, and others involved in wildland fire suppression, there is a website titled "The Smokey Generation." Interviews are listed in the "Stories by Person" link.

Chapter Five

NPRR FORESTER

IN 1864 THE Railway Act granted 200 feet of federal land on either side of the tracks. In addition, odd numbered sections (square miles) 20 miles on either side of the right-of-way to the Northern Pacific Railway (NP) were granted. These lands (40 million acres) would provide federal subsidies for construction of the railroad from Minnesota to the Pacific Ocean.

Much of this land in the west contained timber, which the NP sold. Foresters were hired to lay out the timber sales and designate the trees to be harvested.

My year with the NP was the most physically demanding of my career. I came close to death twice that year. Once when I fell through the ice in the Swan River in 12-below-zero weather, and the other time while dodging falling spruce trees during a wind event. We worked on eight feet of snow that winter, laying out cutting units on snowshoes and marking trees to be cut. Our instructions were that the only times we could stay indoors was if it was colder than thirty below, or if there was a howling blizzard. We had to document the extreme weather condition on our time sheet. We experienced neither one that winter. One morning it was 27-below-zero when we left our cabin. We were hoping our vehicle would start when we returned to it. It did.

Cigars

During 1960, two other men and I, recent graduates from the Missoula Forestry School, were living the first part of the summer in Coil's Motel in Seeley Lake, Montana. The NP was paying the rent.

One of our assignments was to inspect timber sales on NP lands in the Seeley and Swan Valleys for logger compliance with timber utilization requirements. We also inspected erosion control structures installed in temporary roads following their use.

The main logger in the area was Jack Long. (Jack would later own the Caterpillar dealership in Missoula, known as Long's Machinery).

Jack was a large, powerful man, around 6½ feet tall, and appeared to weigh around 250 pounds. By comparison, I was barely 6 feet tall, and weighed a skinny 140 pounds.

One evening I ate a large T-bone steak dinner in Coil's Restaurant and Bar. After dinner, I walked into the bar to have a beer and socialize.

Jack was in the bar, buying beer all around. I thanked him for the beer, and while I was sipping the beer, cigars were passed around. Not being a smoker, I pushed my cigar away.

Jack saw me refuse the cigar, and said, "Light up, Swede."

I thanked Jack for the offer, but stated I did not smoke. Jack then said, "Aw, come on, Swede, light up." I again stated I did not smoke and tried to make myself look smaller than I was.

While looking intently at my beer, I suddenly sensed someone standing next to me. I turned around. There stood Jack, with an evil grin on his face. He said, "LIGHT IT!"

The survival instinct came over me. I lit that cheap cigar! Then I left the bar and threw up that T-bone dinner.

Wind Shear

In the fall of 1960, two other foresters and I were designating timber to be harvested in a thick stand of large spruce trees on NP bottomland in the Swan River drainage in Montana. We were working out of an NP-rented cabin in the Swan Valley.

While we were working, we were hit with a violent wind shear, which started tipping over large shallow-rooted spruce trees located all around us. We were terrified and crawled under a large downed tree to avoid the carnage. The event lasted several minutes, then moved on. We anticipated that the road into the area would be blocked with downed trees. It would be a long walk out.

After crawling over and under fallen trees, we got to our truck and started down the road, no trees had fallen across the road. What luck!

Frozen Malones

In the winter of 1960-61, I, along with three other men, was tasked with designating timber to be harvested on NP land adjacent to the Swan River, in Montana.

When we left our rental cabin one morning, the temperature was around zero. Our plan was to access the area by crossing the ice on the Swan River. This was the easiest way in because a road had not yet been constructed into the proposed timber sale area, which lay on the other side of the river.

We were almost across the ice, when I broke through. I was in water about chest deep. When I pulled myself out of the water, the cold air hit me, and froze my heavy wool Malone trousers board stiff. My 140-pound body was beset by uncontrolled shivering.

I was lucky that I didn't fall through the ice in the middle of the river where the strong under current could have pulled me under the ice. We figured that where I fell through the ice may have been weakened by an underground spring.

We all quickly went ashore and built a huge warming fire in order to warm me and dry out my clothing and boots.

After warming up and drying out, we completed our assignment. With some apprehension, I suspect, we hustled back across the ice and returned to our vehicle.

Busted Nose

In the winter of 1960–61, my "cruising partner" forester Armand Joyce and I were laying out parallel flag (ribbon) lines in timber on NP land in Cold Creek, located in the Swan Valley, Montana. The flag lines were to designate spur roads in preparation for "shovel logging." We were on snowshoes on eight feet of snow. Access into the area was made possible by loggers who were plowing the road in order to log a heavy stand of spruce further up the drainage.

Armand was working upslope from me. Shortly after getting started, I heard Armand in distress. I called to him to ask if he was OK. All I heard was cursing and a garbled reply. I walked up to Armand and saw him sitting down holding a bloody and grossly disfigured nose. It was bent over and resting on his left cheek. He had slid a snowshoe under a windfall. When he tripped, he grabbed a limb to break his fall. The limb bent, then broke, and snapped back and hit him across his nose. He was in great pain and bleeding profusely. I took out my kerchief, filled it with snow, and applied it to his nose in order to stem the bleeding and numb the pain.

We had about a half-hour shuffle in order to return to the truck. I was hoping Armand would not pass out on me.

We made it to the truck, and what followed was an 85-mile trip to Missoula. On arriving at the NP hospital in Missoula, he was referred to a nose physician.

When Armand emerged from the treatment room, he was pale as a ghost. I asked, "Good Lord, Armand, what did he do to you?" Armand said the physician said, "Son, get a good hold of that chair." With that he inserted a stainless-steel prod in one nostril and realigned his nose.

Armand and I retired to the Flame Lounge where we had a couple of drinks. We then drove back to our rental cabin in the Swan.

That night I could hear Armand snuffling and hacking to clear out the mucous and blood draining into his throat. The next morning after breakfast, Armand was back out with me working on snowshoes. That man was tough!

Cruise Mark

In preparation of the timber sales, section (property) lines had to be traced. This involved finding the section (property) corners and designating the connecting property lines.

In order to protect the land ownership monuments (usually a set rock or a pipe with a stamped brass cap), we would "flag" the corners, and chop our "cruise marks" on adjacent trees. These cruise marks were our "calling cards" and faced the monuments so as to facilitate revisiting the property corners.

Our "cruise marks" identified us as NP cruisers. Each cruiser had his own mark. Cruise marks were generally a combination of the first letters in the cruiser's first and last names. Included, and above each mark, was chopped two slant eyes and a nose (called a "monkey face"), which was in respect to the Chinese that built the railroad. Some cruisers added a unique touch to their cruise mark. Jack Winthers would find a small stick in the shape of a pipe and, after adding a mouth to the monkey face, insert the "pipe" in the mouth. The pipe pointed to the monument. Tom Milkey, from Wisconsin, in recognition of his last name, displayed a cow's udder under the monkey face as his cruise mark.

The yin and yang symbol in the center of the NP logo was also in respect to the Chinese.

Nils "Swede" Troedsson's mark

Tom Milkey's mark

FOREST SERVICE EXPERIENCES

I WAS EMPLOYED by the U.S. Forest Service from June 1961 until May 1994. My first two years I was stationed on the Curlew Ranger District, on the Colville National Forest, in northeastern Washington. The balance of my career was on the Beaverhead National Forest, located in southwestern Montana.

Toasted Hardhat

In the fall of 1961, some of us on the forest, including Frank Fowler, (Frank currently resides in Dillon), were dispatched to the Priest Lake Ranger District, on the Kaniksu National Forest in northern Idaho. We were sent there to assist in burning logging slash on a 222-acre clear cut.

The slash was up to six feet deep in most of the area, which included cedar and rotten hemlock. The district claimed that there had recently been two inches of rain. But, down in the depths of the slash, it was still powder dry.

I was instructed to backpack a propane tank and torch mounted on a wooden "clack frame." We started "strip firing" at the top of the clear cut about 5:00 p.m. As soon as an ignition was made, the fire would take off, and we'd have to hustle our way down slope, through deep slash, in order to make the next line of ignitions.

We had been firing about ten minutes when I made another ignition. I turned around to make my way down slope, and I realized I was hemmed in by a huge wall of slash, with the fire starting to leap up behind me. I scrambled to the top of the slash and jumped down. A limb caught the hose on my propane tank, snapping it in half. The hose, under tank pressure, was whipping around, spraying propane gas all around my neck and shoulders. The assistant ranger, who was next to me, shouted to me to run. The survival instinct had already kicked in, and after dropping the tank, I took off running down slope. My hard hat dropped off with the tank, and I didn't even stop to pick it up.

I no sooner got about fifty yards down slope from the tank when there was a huge explosion, followed shortly thereafter by a smaller muffled explosion.

The firing was completed about 7:00 p.m., and I returned home about 2:00 a.m. the next morning.

About a week later I received a package in the mail. The package contained a little blob of aluminum. It was the remains of my hard hat. Included in the package was as a note that surmised that I might like to have it back.

The Priest Lake District had gone back to investigate the accident and found the tank and my hard hat, which I had dropped in a depression. They surmised that the propane gas had settled in the depression and created the first large explosion when it ignited. The second muffled explosion was the soft plug going out of the tank.

Sarsaparilla Bottle

In 1962 I was stationed on the Curlew Ranger District on the Colville National Forest, in northeastern Washington. In advance of laying out a timber sale, located approximately four miles northwest of Curlew, I and a timber technician were walking out section lines and posting metal signs on found section corners. The corners had been established by government surveyors some fifty-plus years previously. Our objectives were to scout the area, and have the signed corners protected by the loggers during logging and road construction.

One day, while walking out a section line, we crossed a stream with a gorgeous meadow straddling it. It was a little before noon, so we broke early so we could sit on the established section line and enjoy the view as we ate our lunch.

While eating our lunch, the technician

The old sarsparilla bottle

noticed the neck of an old bottle sticking out of the "duff." When he pulled it out, the neck was the top of an old bottle. The bottle had turned a light blue with age. The bottle had HOOD'S SARSPARILLA cast on the front of the bottle. On the back of the bottle the word APOTHECARIES was cast. On one edge of the bottle LOWELL MASS was cast, and other edge C.I. HOOD & Co was cast. The bottom of the bottle has the number 59 cast on it. The survey of the rectangular township system began in Washington state in 1851. The survey of this Township was started in 1905. Could the number on the bottom of the bottle indicate the year (1859) the bottle was cast?

The survey party had to cross this stream while they were establishing the section line. They may also have been so impressed with beauty of the area that they stopped to eat lunch here. Might they have left that bottle by the stream when they continued on with their survey?

Today that bottle sits on the fireplace mantel piece in my living room.

Ants

In the summer of 1961, I was stationed on the Curlew Ranger District, on the Colville National Forest, north of Spokane, Washington.

During the summer I was dispatched to the Ash Pile Fire on the Powell Ranger District, on the Clearwater National Forest, in Idaho. The fire was adjacent to the Lochsa River Highway 12, down river from the Powell Ranger Station. Local Dillon, Montana, resident Dan Pence was also on that fire.

I was assigned to a night crew. The fire had gotten into the heart of huge dead cedar trees, which would burn and tip over. Being on line at night and listening to those large cedar trees fall nearby in the dark made for a very tense situation.

Getting a decent rest in camp during the day was impossible. Men were talking and shouting, generators were humming, and vehicles were moving about. To add to the discomfort, the camp was full of ants, which crawled all over you.

The Lochsa River was just across the road from us. In the middle of the river were large, flat rocks. In our desperation to get some decent rest, some of us stripped down to our undershorts and swam out to the flat rocks. There cool air coming off the river, NO ANTS, and the quiet gurgling of the river lulled us to sleep.

I wonder what the tourists thought as they drove by and saw all those men in their undershorts asleep in the middle of the river.

Chain Hoist

From 1961–1963 I was stationed on the on the Colville National Forest, Washington. The District Ranger on the Colville Ranger District was Glen Marriott.

Glen's District had a maintenance shop that was envied by all the other District Rangers. However, Glen's district shop lacked a chain hoist, and he desperately wanted one.

The U.S. Government periodically publishes a list of surplus equipment. A federal agency can acquire surplus items for the cost of the freight. Glen noticed that there was a chain hoist available from the Army base at Fort Lewis, Washington. So, he ordered it.

Sometime later Glen received a call from the Freight Agent at the Tenasket, Washington, rail station. The agent informed Glen that his chain hoist was sitting on a pallet on a railroad flatbed. Glen was advised to arrange for a forklift to load it onto his truck.

The chain hoist was one used to lift tank turrets! Glen only had use for the hoist chain.

Bear Spray

During August 1966, I assisted the Wise River Ranger District in laying out a timber sale in the head of Alder Creek. The two crewmen would stay in the Alder Creek Cabin, located about three miles south of the end of the Bryant Creek Road. My wife, MaryAnn, who accompanied us as a camp cook, and I slept nearby in our tent. We were packed in there by the district packer, Fred Miller.

A black bear had broken into the cabin that previous fall and had gotten into leftover groceries. In the course of consuming the groceries, the bear mixed in a box of dish soap, which cleaned the bear out. The district went in before we occupied the cabin and cleaned the mess up. While there they installed metal brackets above and below each window, and the door. Poles with sharpened bridge spikes could be slipped into the brackets to keep bears out.

In the cabin was a beautiful wood cook stove, which had been skidded in to the cabin on a wooden sled by Assistant Ranger Nevin Guederian, Nevin was assisted by a district crew, and a horse to pull the sled. MaryAnn baked some beautiful pies, loaves of bread, and biscuits in the stove oven. We ate like kings. During the day, while we were gone, a large Stellar Jay would visit MaryAnn for handouts.

I had left a list of groceries at the Wise River Mercantile. The groceries would replenish us during the middle of our sixteen-day stay.

The groceries were packed in by Fred Miller, who stayed for dinner. With a big grin, Fred's dinner-plate-sized hands could fit over three of MaryAnn's biscuits.

On our week end off, we stayed in Alder Creek. On Saturday we hiked into Foolhen Lake to fish. Near the north shore was an old raft. I cut a pole, intent on using it to pole myself out onto lake. As I stepped out onto the grassy bank to get to the raft, I broke through the grass cover and sank up to my waist in peat and mud. That pole was the only thing keeping me from sinking further.

On Sunday, we hiked into Johanna Lake to fish. The fish were long and skinny, from over population, I guess.

As we were packing up at the end of our stay, I came across a can of unused pressurized, non-toxic, orange tree-marking paint. I figured it was payback time for that bear. I coated the can with bacon grease and placed it next to a tree near the cabin.

The next week Nevin visited the cabin and found the paint can with a big chomp mark in it. Orange paint was sprayed all around.

I suspect there was a bear with an orange nose running around the area.

Slapped Down

In the summer of 1994, I was dispatched to Libby, Montana, to supervise a helibase operation that served fires on the Kootenai National Forest.

We were constructing a dip tank that would provide a water source for helicopter buckets.

While we were constructing the dip tank, a Bell 212 helicopter landed close to us. I had my back to the helicopter in order to avoid the strong blast of dust and debris from the rotor wash.

The blast from the rotors picked up a four-foot-by-eight-foot sheet of plywood. It sailed through the air, slapping me on the back with its flat surface. I was knocked to the ground, and lay there, momentarily stunned, with the sheet of plywood on top of me.

Helibase personnel ran over to me, lifted the plywood off of me, and helped me stand up.

I was shaken, but uninjured. It might have turned out different had I been hit with an edge of the plywood sheet.

Watermelon

Shortly before I retired from the Forest Service, I was dispatched to a fire that was near to a small (pop. 200) Alaska village, named Minto. It is located about sixty miles northwest of Fairbanks.

On the way to the fire, we were staged for a couple of days in Ft. Wainwright, near Fairbanks. (The B.L.M. Smokejumper base is headquartered there). There was a "24/7" kitchen on the base. The food was fantastic. I'd visit the kitchen in the middle of the night just to get another helping of halibut!

We flew into Minto in a Twin Otter. We were issued a sheet of visqueen plastic, and mosquito netting. We were instructed to build our individual "hooch." I tried my best to chase out all the buzzing mosquitoes before I went to sleep. When I woke up in the morning there were all kinds of red bellied mosquitoes clinging to the ceiling of my hooch. During the night, they somehow found a way in, and fed on me while I slept.

Shortly after we arrived at the fire, local natives came into our camp selling T-shirts with the name of the fire on them and watermelon for a dollar a pound. One of the local Alaska fire fighters wondered how the fire got started. He stated that there had been no lightning in the area for two weeks. I suspected the fire couldn't get started until a Twin Otter landed with the T-shirt and watermelon order.

Shortly thereafter, I heard that the Alaska Fire Service established a policy that no native who lived within fifty miles of a fire would be hired on. I wonder if the policy resulted in a reduction in the frequency of man-caused fires.

The common joke I heard about Alaska was that the state bird was the mosquito and the state flower was the abandoned fifty-five-gallon fuel drum. My perception was that the natives were quite careless with the landscape. Abandoned snowmobiles, fuel drums, worn out stoves, refrigerators, furniture, and other trash littered the tundra.

One evening I went over to the heavy equipment operator camp to visit. There was a dozer operator there, wearing glasses with thick, greasy lenses. He was wearing a dirty cap with the name Blue Moon Saloon, Cameron, Montana, on it. Small world. He had come to Alaska from Montana to work on the pipeline. When that project was finished, he was drifting from job to job.

The Alaska assignment was a real education for me.

A Good Crew

In the summer of 1968, I was stationed on the Beaverhead National Forest, headquartered in Dillon, Montana.

I was assigned a crew of eight summer temporary employees. Most were college students and good conscientious young men. We were tasked with measuring sample timber plots on the Gravelly and Madison Mountain Ranges, and later, on the Magruder Corridor in Idaho. I suspect this was in conjunction with areas being proposed for wilderness designation. We were assigned a Bell 47G helicopter to help transport us to the more remote areas.

We were provided four brand-new pickup trucks from a Ford dealership in Bozeman. The forest Administrative Officer (AO) cautioned me not to damage the trucks, as the process to settle damage claims was a real inconvenience. In spite of the AO's instructions, the accidents started:

One of my crewmen had a flat on one of the front four-ply tires. In his haste to jack up the front end with a tall handyman jack, he failed to notice the hood rose up against a wire stretcher protruding from the top of the jack. Needless to say, a crimp was put in the hood.

On a hot July weekend, one of my crewmen left his pack in the cab of the pickup. The buildup of heat in the cab caused a bottle of bug repellent to leak out and melt a hole in the seat cover.

One late July day I got a radio request from the Forest Dispatcher to board the patrol plane which was being dispatched to the Sportsman's Lodge airfield in Ennis. The request was for me to check on a fire that had been reported in Hyde Creek (Hyde Creek flows into the Wall Creek Wildlife Management Area, approximately 30 miles south of Ennis.)

Upon arriving over the fire, I reported that it was really taking off. It was then I noticed one of my rental pickups approaching out of a cloud of dust. I was unable to communicate with the driver to caution him not to try drive up the very rough road up the Hyde Creek ridge. Up the road he charged, sliding to a stop within a foot of a tree lying across the road. The driver (not one of my crewmen) jumped out of the truck, grabbed a Pulaski, and started chopping furiously on the tree. He missed the tree with one of his swings and stuck the Pulaski into the hood of the truck! I was watching all of this from the aircraft, thinking OOPS!

In August we were sent to the Magruder Corridor to measure sample plots there.

One evening I drove out to a helispot to pick up a couple of my crewmen who were arriving in our assigned helicopter. The first crewman got out of the idling helicopter. As the second crewman got out, he retrieved his pack from the cargo rack. As he threw the pack over his shoulder, a can of pressurized orange tree marking paint fell on the ground.

He intended to throw out from under the rotating blades. Instead, it went up into the main rotor, exploding, and covering the ship's bubble and main rotor with paint.

The pilot immediately shut down to check the main rotor for damage. There was a slight nick in one of the blades, but the helicopter was still flyable.

The mechanic spent a good part of that evening cleaning the paint off the aircraft.

At the end of the summer, the crew gave me a beautiful fishing creel in appreciation for maintaining my good sense of humor and looking out for their welfare.

All in all, it was a fun summer.

Gatorade

I retired from the U.S. Forest Service in May 1994. For four or five years following my retirement I continued to be dispatched to fires as a State of Montana employee. My usual assignment was as an Air Support Supervisor, managing logistics and support personnel for the aviation program.

In the summer following my retirement, I was dispatched to a Bureau of Management (BLM) fire 35 miles southwest of Ely, Nevada. My duty was supervising helicopter operations.

The weather was extremely hot. We had a Bell 212 helicopter that, during the heat of the afternoon, could only carry two passengers to our helispot located above 9,000 feet. (At lower elevations, on a cool day, this helicopter could carry a dozen fire fighters.)

On the helibase we had two garbage cans filled with ice, soft drinks, and Gatorade. We were flying cold Gatorade and soft drinks to the fire line. Fire fighters arriving at the helibase at the end of their shift were dehydrated. They would slug down a liter of Gatorade on their walk up to camp. After several days, we noticed that fire fighters were bypassing diet soft drinks. They preferred drinks containing a high concentration of sugar, and Gatorade.

The last morning, I was at the helibase, we were informed we could sleep in. No crews could be flown out to the fire line. We could hear a din of slamming porta potty doors. Forty percent of the crews had diarrhea!

I was released from the fire that morning without finding out what was causing the sickness. None of us on the helibase got sick. I left wondering if we on the helibase had caused the illness. We had failed to dump Clorox into the garbage cans in order to kill any germs from fire fighters dipping their dirty hands into the cans in order to retrieve a drink.

The next summer I encountered the Ely BLM helitack foreman on a fire in California. I asked him what caused the sickness the previous summer on the fire south of Ely. He informed me that they had called in the Nevada Department of Health to investigate. They checked the drinking water, the caterer, and camp sanitation. They finally determined it was the Gatorade. Firefighters were drinking too much of it undiluted. It was setting off their electrolytes and "flushing them out."

Flicker Vertigo

One summer, before I retired from the U.S. Forest Service in 1994, I was dispatched to a fire in the Salmon River country in Idaho. My assignment was managing a helibase.

One afternoon a fire fighter exited from a helicopter at our helibase, and he immediately began throwing up. I went over to him to inquire as to what was his problem. He informed me that he has epilepsy, and the flicker from the rotating rotor blades had made him sick. He called the phenomenon "flicker vertigo." He said it could trigger an epileptic seizure.

He had failed to mention that he has epilepsy when he hired on. He was immediately released from the fire and returned to his home unit.

Sometime later I was informed that some who have epilepsy are reluctant to enter a room with rotating ceiling fans. The flickering shadows from the blades could send them into a seizure. Dr. Ron Loge states, "The flickering certainly can trigger a seizure in someone who is prone to it but not with everyone who has epilepsy. It also depends on the frequency. Strobe lights and TV flickering can also be triggers."

Zero 2 Tango

During the period 1975–1990, my duties on the Beaverhead National Forest (BNF) included supervising the forest aviation program. This assignment included administering the contract with the Dillon Flying Service, who provided aircraft and pilots for fire detection flights, transportation of our personnel to assignments on fires, and administrative flights for resource specialists, and Rangers.

Our personnel in Wise River who were dispatched to distant fires, or needed an aircraft for administrative flights, had to drive to Butte to get on an aircraft. With this inconvenience in mind, I felt it desirable to have an airport in Wise River.

Rancher Don Jones owned a field adjacent to the Pioneer Scenic Byway, about five miles south of Wise River. Don had been a private pilot and aircraft owner.

With the support of Wise River District Ranger Ed Levert, and local resident Ron Primozic, we got Don to lease 45 acres to Beaverhead County for 50 years for $10.

Ed arranged for the Anaconda Job Corps to construct the airfield as a heavy equipment operator training opportunity for their students. Under a permit, fill (soil) was obtained from B.L.M. land adjacent to the airport. This fill was used to provide a cushion layer over rocky ground for the construction of the 4,050-foot-long runway, taxiway, and tie down area. Materials for tie downs were donated by Vigilante Electric. The construction was supervised by Dillon resident Richard Miller, who worked for the Job Corps at the time. In response to concerns expressed by the FAA, boulders adjacent to the runway were reduced to rubble by a Forest Service explosive blaster recertification class.

The Forest Service provided the engineering, the archeologist for the required site survey, and the backhoe with operator to install the tie downs. The Job Corps constructed the airfield in the summer of 1988 and became operational in late 1988. The windsock "standard" (pole) came from the abandoned airfield in Jackson.

The Job Corps donated a vault toilet. The Montana Aeronautics Division (MAD) offered on the ground advice and donated the windsock. A "toll disconnect" telephone was installed inside, which limited telephone calls to the local area. Pilots could call a local cafe for a ride into town and back, so long as they purchased a meal.

An enameled telephone sign for outside the toilet came from the Philipsburg Airfield. A fly swatter was hung next to the toilet riser, with a sign that read "For Unreported Traffic." The airfield was approved by the M.A.D. and the FAA and was assigned the "designator" 02T. The airport approval included the use by DC-3s and Twin Otters.

Dodging Cranes

I thought it would be desirable to have access to some airfields approved for our use along the south rim of our forest. These could be used for aircraft support to fires, rescue, or other administrative activities in the area.

In the late 1970s I requested that a Forest Service pilot fly down from Missoula to inspect airports located in the Centennial Valley, Horse Prairie, the Red Rock Lakes National Wildlife Refuge (NWR), and Raynolds Pass, just north of Henry's Lake, and adjacent to Highway 87.

Pilot Bob Nicol flew down in a Cessna 206 with a STOL (Short Takeoff Or Landing) kit to inspect the airports. The airport on the north side of the Centennial Valley, near Metzel Creek , was owned by Byron Martinell, and was approved for our use. (It was later used during a back-country rescue. This was mentioned in the story Primate Pills). The airport in Horse Prairie was owned by John Morse, and was approved for our use, as were the airports near Raynolds Pass, and on the NWR.

The airport on the south side of the Centennial Valley was owned by Sam Brenneman, a rancher, and former pilot and aircraft owner. The runway was bordered on both sides by marsh and scrub land, and appeared to be smooth, with adequate length. As we flared to land, about a dozen sand hill cranes jumped out of their nests in panic and crossed back and forth in front of us. We threaded our way through them, almost colliding with one. After landing, we exited the aircraft. We could hear a cacophony of crane calls from their nests adjacent to the runway. Hitting one of those BIG birds may have ended our flying that day.

Our departure was the shortest takeoff possible! This airport WAS NOT approved for our use.

Pictographs

In the early part of the 1990s, the Dillon Ranger District wildlife biologist Stacey Courville and I were on patrol west of Lima. Our objective was to contact hunters just prior to the opening of the general hunting season in order to explain Forest Service travel restrictions, sell them maps, and answer questions about the area.

Stacey was from St. Ignatius, Montana, and proud of his Native American heritage. He was an "enrolled" member of his local tribe (Salish-Kootenai).

As we were about to turn off the Little Sheep Creek Road, and drive up to the East Creek Camp Ground, I asked Stacey if he was aware that there were some pictographs on the bluff just on the other side of East Creek and behind an old cabin. Stacey said he was not aware. I suggested he grab his camera, and we'd go have a look.

We hopped across the creek, and Stacey commenced to take photographs of the pictographs. As Stacey was taking photographs, I explained that it was my understanding that they had been painted by the local Tendoy Indians.

I thought I would test Stacey's sense of humor. I went on to falsely claim that it was my understanding that the local Indians would gather into a raiding party each year and ride up into the Flathead Valley, fight the local Indians, and steal their horses and women.

I turned around to check Stacey's reaction. He had an evil grin on his face and said, "Not on their best day!"

Llamas

For nine years in a row during the 1980s, I was a Forest Service aerial observer during the opening weekend of the General Hunting Season. I would coordinate with personnel on the ground monitoring hunter activities in the Gravelly and Snowcrest Mountain Ranges. This area is located south of Virginia City, Montana. My main responsibility was to detect and report violations of our off-road motorized travel restrictions.

Montana Game Warden Jim DeBoer participated in our activities, as well as enforcing state big game hunting regulations. He carried one of our portable radios in order to coordinate with us, and so we could contact him when we discovered a hunting violation.

One opening day a Madison Ranger District officer asked me to check activity in Eureka Basin, which is on the south end of the Gravelly Mountains.

After flying over the area and checking the Basin, I informed the officer that the only activity I observed was two hunters hunting with llamas.

Jim came on the air and said that persons of any religious persuasion were permitted to hunt in the area.

Mooned

On May 22, 2020, on the morning TV news on KXLF (Butte), a photo was displayed of three pelicans tipped forward and looking underwater for food. Their hind ends were facing the camera. The photo was titled "Pelican moon." This reminded me of when I was "mooned."

In 1976, Bill Werhane (MSO-66) requested that I present an hour lecture on back country rescue to returning Smokejumpers. The presentation was in the Conference Room in the Missoula Smokejumper Base dormitory.

Behind the Conference Room was a small coffee room. The door to the coffee room was open. As I was delivering my lecture in front of the group, Jim Scofield (MSO-66), the Regional Helicopter Specialist, entered the coffee room behind the class. He'd been out running. and was still in his sweat suit.

After giving me a big evil grin, he turned, dropped his sweatpants, and mooned me. The group, their backs to him, was unaware of what was going on. I smiled and continued my lecture.

Later that day I was relating this incident to Nels Jensen (MSO-62), the Regional Aviation Officer. Nels laughed, and related the following mooning story to me:

On final approach to the Silver City Airport, New Mexico, he was piloting a Beech Baron, having returned from a lead plane mission. As he was taxiing to the Smokejumper parachute loft, a Southwest Airlines Boeing 737 passenger jet was taxiing to the terminal. At the same time, a DC-3 jump plane was roaring down the runway on its way to a fire. As it passed by the loft, a "pair of hams" was pressed against each window facing the loft. In front of the loft a group of jumpers mooned back at them. Boys will be boys!

Heavy Load

From 1965 to 1994, I was stationed in the Beaverhead National Forest Supervisor's Office in Dillon. My main duty was assisting ranger districts in timber sale preparation and administration.

Late one fall in the 1970s, I was assisting Ray Franks, the Jackson District Assistant Ranger, in laying out a timber sale in Dry Creek. Dry Creek is just north of Big Lake Creek, in the West Big Hole.

I happened to mention to the forest wildlife biologist, Mike Rath, that we had seen a lot of fresh elk sign in the proposed sale area. Mike got excited and wanted to take annual leave and return with us to hunt elk in the area.

The next day Mike and I drove from Dillon, picked up Ray at the Jackson Ranger Station, and returned to Dry Creek. We split up, Ray and I working on preparing the sale, and Mike taking off to hunt elk. By mid-afternoon we heard a rifle shot north of us. When we caught up with Mike, he told us that he was squatted down, "taking care of business," when a cow elk wandered by him. He shot the elk.

We assisted Mike in dressing out and quartering the elk. It was a little over a mile to the truck. After lashing a front quarter to a Kelty pack frame, we took turns packing each one to the truck. By the time we got the second quarter to the truck, daylight was fading fast. Desperate to beat the dark, we returned to the kill site and lashed BOTH hind quarters onto the pack frame. Mike and I could only walk about 500 yards with the heavy load before we had to switch off. We placed the load on Ray. Ray went about 50 yards and collapsed. Ray, a 120 pound pin butt, was pinned to the ground by the load. We picked up the load off Ray, and Mike and I completed the pack out.

When we returned to the ranger station, we weighed the last load on a spring scale in the warehouse. It weighed 117 pounds! My thighs were sore for several days afterward.

Shortly thereafter, I wrote a letter to the Kelty company requesting some parts for the pack frame. In the letter I mentioned our elk pack out and stated that their pack frame held up a lot better than we did.

The Kelty company replied, thanking me for my letter, and included, free of charge, the parts I had requested. I wonder if my letter ended up being posted on the company bulletin board.

Oreo Cookies

In the summer of 1988, while working for the U.S. Forest Service, I was dispatched to the Truman Gulch fire on the west side of the Bridger Mountain Range, Montana. My assignment was as an Air Support Group Supervisor.

Helicopters were dipping water out of the Bridger Bowl Ski Area settling ponds. The ski area is on the east side of the Bridger Range. The pilots complained that as they were lifting the bucket loads of water over the Bridger Range, they encountered the prevailing wind spilling over the ridge. This created a dangerous down draft.

Near our helibase was a ranch with a deep stock water pond. I contacted the Procurement Unit Leader on the fire to see if we could negotiate a procurement agreement which would allow our helicopters to dip out of the pond. He agreed, and we drove to the ranch.

The knock on the door was answered by a woman. She appeared to be VERY pregnant, and had a toddler hanging on to her skirt. We explained the reason for our visit, and she invited us in. She said her husband was out doing chores and would return shortly. She offered us coffee and cookies while we waited. The place appeared to be quite bare.

When she opened the cupboard to get the cookies, I noticed there was hardly anything in the cupboard. She brought out what I suspected was the last of her Oreo Cookies.

Eventually her husband appeared. He was rail thin, and his clothes were well patched. He agreed to a procurement agreement that would allow our helicopters to dip out of his pond. The Procurement Unit Leader said he would return with a proposed agreement.

On our drive back to the fire camp, the Procurement Unit Leader asked me if $25/day was a fair offer. I pointed out the potential savings each helicopter would incur on each trip by not having to lift their water buckets over the ridge. In fact, at least $200 would be saved on each trip.

Not only that, the safety risk the pilots were complaining about would be mitigated. I suggested that this dip site was worth at least $200 for each day that the helicopters dipped out of the pond, and that the agreement should be left open until Christmas in case the fire popped up again.

The Procurement Unit Leader agreed and returned to the ranch house to get the agreement signed. During the days following, every time the rancher went by our helibase, he would grin and wave to us.

I felt the government's money was well spent.

Sky Cranes

In 1991, I was assigned as Air Support on the Thompson Creek Fire. The fire was south of Livingston, Montana. Dude ranches and summer day camps were threatened.

The evening prior to my dispatch, on the TV news, I watched as day camp children were being evacuated on school buses. I anticipated the dispatch, so I packed my red fire pack.

The fire grew into a large "project" fire. We had fifteen helicopters, which included a Sky Crane, and several Montana Air National Guard helicopters. The helicopters were burning in excess of 25,000 gallons of Jet A fuel every day. A jet fuel bulk dealer from Bozeman parked a large fuel truck at the helibase and let the helicopter crews sign for the fuel. With seven spike camps to supply with helicopters, I had over 150 personnel, including helicopter crews, in my helibase organization. I ordered a Deputy Air Support and a Deputy Helibase Manager to assist us in this extremely busy helicopter operation.

A retired Southwest Airlines luggage handler had signed on and was assigned to the helicopter cargo ("Heli cargo") operation. At a morning briefing, in jest, I introduced the retired baggage handler. I advised the helicargo personnel to keep an eye on him to make sure cargo was flown to the proper spike camps.

As the fire wound down, the Sky Crane was released to return to Oregon. It flew into the Livingston Airport to top off fuel for the flight back home. The Sky Crane pilot asked the FBO (Fixed Base Operator) if he could "hot fuel." The FBO approved, so the pilot taxied up to the pump to take on fuel with engines still running.

After about ten minutes, the FBO felt a tap on his shoulder. He turned around. It was the pilot telling him to shut it down. The Sky Crane was burning the fuel faster than the FBO could pump it in. (The Sky Crane burns over 500 gallons per hour.)

The Sky Crane departed the Livingston airport, and flew to the Bozeman Airport to finish topping off its fuel.

In 1994 I was assigned to the Kootenai Complex Fires as an Air Support Group Supervisor. The Kootenai National Forest had sustained a record lighting storm. Two spotter aircraft were launched. There was so many lightening fires, that eventually the smoke grew so thick the aerial observers could no longer spot the fires, so they had to land.

A Sikorsky S-64 Sky Crane was assigned to one of the fires. It was sucking water out of a lake with a recently developed "snorkel" system. The lake was in the Libby municipal watershed. On its last trip, the pilots could not shut off the pump, and the Sky Crane slowly settled into the lake. The pilot and copilot had to swim to shore.

Elk Wrestling

For about eight years during the 1980s, about forty of us with the Forest Service, the Bureau of Land Management, and husky college students, would assist Montana Fish, Wildlife and Parks big game biologists in their elk drive netting program. This program was held in April in the Wall Creek and Blacktail Wildlife Management Areas (WMAs).

A helicopter would drive elk into two rows of nets held upright with poles. We would jump on the entangled elk, wrestle them to the ground, and blindfold them to quiet them down. A veterinarian would then scan the cows' bellies with a portable ultrasound to determine if they were pregnant. Blood samples were collected from the pregnant cows, and age determined through tooth examination.

The blood samples would later be examined in a Bozeman lab to check for disease and to verify pregnancy. Pregnant cows would be fitted with a radio collar. They could later be individually checked by radio from an aircraft to see if they had a calf by their side. This would help biologists monitor "recruitment" percentage.

In 1989 we were drive netting elk in the Blacktail WMA. Ron Schott, the Madison District Assistant Ranger, was lying down between the rows of nets. A cow elk came charging through the net above him and headed straight towards him. Ron jumped up to get out of the way. The elk slammed into him, dislocating Ron's left shoulder. Dan Pence, a local Forest Service employee, helped me load Ron into the helicopter. Ron and I were flown into Dillon, landing near the hospital emergency room entrance.

There we were, standing in our insulated Carhart coveralls, covered with elk hair. I had to explain several times to amazed medical personnel how Ron got his shoulder dislocated.

The hospital personnel could not reduce Ron's dislocation because his shoulder muscles were so tensed up. He was sent to the St. James Hospital in Butte where his dislocated shoulder was reduced.

That fall Ron was bow hunting elk. When he drew his bow to shoot a six-point bull elk, his shoulder dislocated! The elk ran off. He had to straddle a log until his shoulder muscles relaxed, and his dislocated shoulder reduced itself. What followed was corrective surgery in Butte to permanently stabilize the shoulder.

Drive netting elk with helicopter
Photo courtesy Pete Bengeyfield

Flies

In the latter part of my career with the U.S. Forest Service, I attended six weeks of Continuing Education in Fire Management. Three weeks were spent at the university in Missoula, Montana, and three weeks were spent at the university in Moscow, Idaho.

The fire professor in Missoula was Ron Wakamoto. Our class was attended by about twenty Forest Service employees who were well into their careers. Whenever the class deteriorated into a B.S. session, it was usually about guns, hunting, or fishing.

One day Ron was telling us about a call he got from a friend of his. His friend had purchased a rifle at a gun show. It was a heavy-barreled Sako chambered for a .22-250 Remington, with a large telescopic sight, and a Timney single-stage trigger. When you pushed the trigger forward, a 3-ounce touch would set it off.

Ron's friend stated that the rifle was unbelievably accurate and invited Ron out to the local rifle range the coming Saturday so he could witness the accuracy.

That Saturday they drove out to the rifle range. Ron's friend set up the rifle on the bench rest, and rough sighted it to the 100 yard back stop. They then walked up to the backstop, and Ron's friend tacked up a target. The target center was a solid black circle, with about a dime-sized white center. His friend then unscrewed the lid off a little jar, which contained fresh dog feces, and smeared the white center with the dog feces.

They then returned to the bench rest. His friend chambered a round, pushed the trigger forward, and centered the cross hairs on the target. He kept peeking through the scope. Pretty soon, BZZZZ, a fly landed on the dog feces. His friend squeezed the trigger. BOOM, SPLAT! Ron's friend now had a witness who could vouch for the fact that he could kill flies at 100 yards with that rifle!

TFR

In the latter part of my Forest Service career I was dispatched as an Air Support Group Supervisor to a fire on the Lewis & Clark National Forest. The fire was in the Castle Mountains, southeast of White Sulphur Springs, MT.

A Temporary Flight Restriction (TFR) was filed with the FAA, which prohibited sightseeing and non-essential aircraft from entering the designated air space around the fire. This was to protect the five helicopters and air tankers fighting our fire.

One morning, during our crew shuttle operations, on a command net radio, I overheard a Crew Concepts helicopter pilot, flying a Bell 212, complaining that a Super Cub was threading its way through our helicopters delivering fire fighters to the fire line. I asked the pilot if the Cub had a funny-looking antenna under one wing. The pilot confirmed the presence of the antennae and stated that he had chased the Cub out of the area by descending down on it. The Cub pilot saw the shadow of the 212 on the ground underneath him and immediately left the area.

The antennae under the Cub wing led me to suspect that it was a local big-game biologist checking to see if the local radio-collared elk herd had been displaced by the fire activity.

A follow-up confirmed my suspicions. The local Montana Fish, Wildlife and Parks (MFWP) big game biologist had gotten permission to enter our air space from the Forest Dispatch Office in Great Falls. The dispatcher never checked with us to see if there was a potential for conflict. The incident was caused by our failure, not by the failure of the MFWP big-game biologist.

Fortune Cookie

In May 1994, a Forest Service personnel specialist was filling out my retirement papers. I was completing over thirty-five years of service to the U.S. Government.

We hadn't quite completed the paperwork at noon, so we broke for lunch. I took my wife down to the local Chinese restaurant here in Dillon, Montana.

At the completion of lunch, I broke open a fortune cookie. On the slip of paper was printed "It's time for a change." The personnel specialist felt the message so appropriate she placed a copy of it in my retirement folder.

Chapter Seven

CANOEING WITH WARDENS

I RETIRED IN Dillon, Montana, from the Forest Service in 1994. Not too long thereafter, I was approached by local Game Warden Mike Mehn with a request that I take him on a canoe trip in the Chain of Lakes to enforce fishing and water safety regulations. These lakes are located on the Beaverhead–Deerlodge National Forest, on the north side of the Centennial Valley. What followed was day and overnight canoe trips with four different wardens. I was happy to do this on a volunteer basis.

On August 8, 1998, Mike and I set camp in a secluded area just south of Hidden Lake. The plan was that the next day we would check fishermen on Hidden, Goose, and Otter Lakes.

Dinner that night started with "G&T" drinks, followed by a garden salad, charcoal broiled catfish filets that had been marinated in white wine and soy sauce, and sprinkled with lemon pepper. This was accompanied by steamed corn on the cob, and steamed broccoli slathered with hollandaise sauce. All of this was washed down with cold beer. Dessert was strawberry shortcake with whipped cream. The evening was concluded with coffee. The coffee was made by pouring hot water over coffee grounds in a filter set in a Malita˚ coffee filter holder mounted on a mason jar. Mike states: "—boy we ate good."

Breakfast the next morning was blueberry hotcakes covered with warm maple syrup that had butter melted in it. In addition to the hotcakes I served bacon, eggs, and mason-jar coffee.

All the fishermen checked on Hidden Lake were legal. We then portaged my 14-foot Kevlar canoe (34 pounds) to Goose Lake, about one mile north of Hidden Lake.

On the way to Goose Lake, we heard some people approaching us. Mike handed me the canoe and hid in nearby brush. I took over portaging the canoe and met two couples headed for Hidden Lake. Playing dumb (easy for a Swede) I asked them if this was the way to Cliff Lake, two miles north of us. They said it was and said they were staying at the Cliff Lake Resort. They looked at each other, shook their heads in disbelief, and continued on to Hidden Lake.

As we approached Goose Lake, we observed what appeared to be an outfitter's camp at the outlet. Six horses were picketed close to the camp. Two men were leaving camp, headed for Otter Lake, about a quarter mile north of us. Commercial outfitting in this area was prohibited by the Forest Service.

On our approach to Otter Lake, we observed the two fishermen we had seen leaving camp. They were fishing on the east side of the lake.

A man and boy were on the west side of the lake. The man dashed into some brush, to hide a fishing pole, I suspect. Mike approached the two men. They were from Pennsylvania and had the proper fishing licenses.

They explained that they had "booked" with the man on the other side of the lake. The man was a real estate realtor from Ogden, Utah. He had borrowed the horses from his Dad who owned a ranch near Henry's Lake, Idaho. They had ridden the horses into Montana and across the Centennial Valley to Goose Lake.

I asked the men if they would like their picture taken with a Montana Game Warden. I offered to send them copies. They were eager to have the photo and I took it.

Mike then interviewed the outfitter and found out he was not licensed to outfit in Montana. (Also, I suspect, he did not have a Forest Service Special Use Permit). Mike told the outfitter he would visit further with him in his camp. I suggested to Mike that he follow the outfitter, and I would portage the canoe back to Goose Lake.

When I arrived at Goose Lake, Mike was in a serious discussion with the illegal outfitter. Mike ordered the outfitter to break camp the next day and return to Idaho. I took photos of the camp and horses before we headed back to Hidden Lake.

On our way back to Hidden Lake, Mike was portaging the canoe. Halfway back we encountered the two women we had run into earlier. One of the women noticed the warden patch on Mike's sleeve. She said: "Oh, I forgot the truck keys," and started running back to Hidden Lake. Mike handed me the canoe and quickly followed after her. He found two California men fishing without licenses. The woman had not reached them in time to warn them. He cited both men for "fishing without."

On our way out to our vehicle, I mentioned to Mike that I suspected the outfitter crossed into Montana without a livestock inspection.

When I returned to Dillon, I gave copies of the six photos I had taken to Mike, the Montana Livestock Inspector in Dillon, and to the Forest Service Law Enforcement Officer in Ennis.

Mice *by Kerry Wahl*

The following is from an E-mail sent 7/1/20 to me by Montana Fish, Wildlife and Parks (FWP) Game Warden Kerry Wahl. It was in response to my story titled Rats. This story is shared with Kerry's approval:

"Man, I like this story and hate it at the same time. Why? My first 9 years with FWP were spent in a house on the Rosebud Battlefield south of Busby built in 1909. I was the first ever Park Ranger FWP hired for the Tongue River State Park. The outside walls were stucco to keep it from leaning over time. Before I got there, the previous resident's wife shot a skunk that got in the living room and that carpet was never removed! The mice were terrible in that house. I had a running trap line throughout and included small boxes of poison here and there. I killed an awful lot of mice over the years! My last summer there I nailed 27 mice in my kitchen and living room. I still remember the number 22 years later! That didn't count the ones dying from poison. All the mice would attract rattlesnakes to the yard, and I had to shotgun a few outside the house and my dog damn near got bit twice. This part of the 90s also brought about the Hantavirus down in New Mexico. I heard about it in a newspaper article and immediately got concerned because of all the mice in and around the house. Then some folks in Montana got it and died from it. That was one house that could have easily had Hantavirus, but maybe I became immune to it from living there. When I left the house in 1998, I struggled not to light it on fire and never look back. Good story Swede and thanks for writing it although I've got my own bad memories, ha!"

The Livestock Inspector took the photos to Idaho, where he met up with the Idaho Livestock Inspector. It appears the illegal outfitter had ridden back into Idaho without a livestock inspection.

I suspect the illegal outfitter didn't make much money on that trip. I wonder if he was an Idaho licensed outfitter. Oh, by the way, I did send the Pennsylvania fishermen copies of the photo taken of them standing alongside Mike. They never thanked me. (Neither fisherman was cited for having booked with an unlicensed Montana outfitter).

Following the canoe trips with Mike, I volunteered to take three other Game Wardens on canoe trips to enforce fishing and water safety regulations.

Warden Mike Mehn checking a "tuber" on Hidden Lake

Warden DeBoer in Axolotl Lakes Camp

Warden DeBoer cooking blueberry hotcakes

"Swede" Troedsson portaging canoe from Axolotl Lake
Photo courtesy Perry Backus

Axolotls
Photo courtesy Perry Backus

Cow moose at Axolotl Lake
Photo courtesy Perry Backus

Cow moose at Axolotl Lake
Photo courtesy Perry Backus

Elk Skeleton

In June 1996, Warden Mike Mehn and I were canoeing on Hidden Lake, located on the north side of the Centennial Valley in southwest Montana. We were there to check on fishermen.

We stopped on the east shore to pick up trash left by campers. Next to the abandoned camp was the skeleton of a large bull elk. The elk appeared to have died the previous winter. The antlers and elk ivory teeth were missing. Imbedded in the vertebra was an arrowhead. The shaft was broken off.

The angle of the arrow suggests an uphill shot entered under the rib and lodged in the spine. We speculate that the wounded elk was shot on the bench above the lake and made its way down to the lake to be near water, where it died.

Later a Dillon large animal veterinarian informed me that she estimated that the calcium callus (growth around the arrowhead) took 6 to 8 weeks to form.

 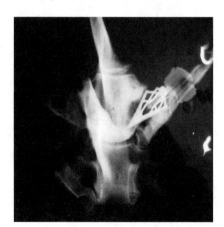

The elk spine and an x-ray of the imbedded arrowhead

Chapter Eight

HUNTING

Goat Hunt

FOR MOST OF my career with the U.S. Forest Service, I was stationed in the Beaverhead National Forest Supervisor's office in Dillon, Montana. My main duty was assisting ranger districts with their timber program.

Due to my knowledge of the area, the receptionist would often refer hunters' inquiries to me.

One fall, just prior to the opening of the mountain goat hunting season, a phone call from a Butte resident was switched to me. The caller was an Army Sergeant with the recruiting office. He had a goat permit for the East Pioneer Mountains area and wanted some advice as to where to hunt. I informed him that I also had a goat permit for the same area, and suggested we hook up and hunt together. He gladly accepted the invitation.

The day prior to opening of the season, we made camp in a stringer meadow located just above Trapper Lake. Trapper Lake is located 1½ miles south of the old abandoned mining town of Hecla. (Hecla is approximately 12 miles WSW of Melrose). We spent the afternoon looking the area over. During our "area recon," I showed him an old goat trap that had been established by Montana Fish, Wildlife and Parks in a saddle above, and west of Hecla.

The next day we spent the day looking for mountain goats. We had no luck, but we found plenty of goat hair. The weather was gorgeous, and we enjoyed scrambling around the beautiful area. The sergeant was a little overweight, but surprisingly in good shape.

The next week the sergeant asked me to go hunting with him again. I could not go because of a social commitment. Monday morning the sergeant called me to relate his hunting success over the weekend.

The sergeant was ready to leave his office Friday afternoon when his Captain inquired as to the sergeant's plans for the weekend. The sergeant replied that he was planning to hunt goats. The Captain laughed and said he just could not picture this "fat boy" hunting goats.

The sergeant tore out of his office and arrived at the goat trap just after the end of shooting light. There was a big billy goat lapping up snow melt water in the trap.

Early the next morning the sergeant sneaked up to the goat trap in the dark. At daybreak, there was the billy goat again, drinking water in the trap. He shot the goat, dressed it out, and slid it into his four-wheel drive van. He was back in Butte by noon.

When the Captain arrived at his office Monday, there was a goat scrotum on his desk. Attached was a note that said, "From the fat boy."

Elk Retreival

One evening, in early December, as my wife and I were preparing dinner, we heard a knock on our kitchen door. Ken and Cathy Heffner, local Forest Service employees, were standing in the doorway dressed in hunting clothes. I invited them inside and asked them what was up.

Cathy had a late season cow elk permit for an area south of Ennis, and east of the Madison River. They had been hunting east of Highway 287 when a game warden informed them that a group of elk had crossed the highway and were headed for the river.

Ken and Cathy hustled down towards the river. Cathy wounded a cow. The cow ran into the river and bedded down on an island of soft ice in the middle of the river. Cathy put a finishing shot into the elk but had no way to get to it to tag and dress it out.

I asked Ken if he was leading up to an invitation to help them retrieve the elk with my canoe. Ken sheepishly said yes. I told Ken that my wife and I had planned to go to Butte the next day. She would purchase a wedding band for me with waitress tips she'd been saving for six months. I pointed to two domestic ducks defrosting on the counter and to a bottle of wine. Our plan was to celebrate when we returned home. I could see Ken and Cathy were quite embarrassed. I told Ken I needed to check with my wife.

My wife said, "Go ahead." I told Ken and Cathy I would help them provided they would help us eat those ducks and drink that wine when we got home. They were OK with that.

I called local game warden Sarge Hoem and explained the situation to him. We were going after an untagged elk, and if a warden wanted to accompany us, he was welcome. Sarge said "Just get it done." I also told Sarge I wondered if we were going after a sour elk. Sarge said in the late Gardiner hunts he had seen killed elk go thirty-five hours before being dressed out, and they came out fine.

The next morning, we all had a blueberry hotcake breakfast at my home. Then we hooked up my trailer to my Bronco, lashed the canoe onto the roof rack, and headed for the Madison.

The wind was howling in the Madison Valley. When we drove into a BLM campground, Ken focused his binoculars on the ice island and said, "There it is." I focused my binoculars on the island and told Ken all I saw was grass sticking out of the ice. Ken said, "Swede, that's not grass, that's elk hair." During the night the elk had sunk into the soft ice.

Ken and I put on our hip boots and unloaded the canoe. The river was shallow enough that we were able to safely wade out to the elk by using the canoe to steady ourselves.

Upon arriving at the elk, Ken attempted to lift the elk onto the ice so we could dress it out, quarter it, and load the quarters into the canoe. In spite of Ken being a big and powerful man, he could not lift the elk onto the ice. I let go of the canoe to give him a hand. The wind blew it off the island and down the river. The canoe, pushed by the wind and current, kept slamming into the west bank and shooting out into the river. About one-half mile below us, the river turned to the west. The canoe crashed into the east bank, slid up onto the top of the bank, and stopped!

We towed the whole elk back across the river, intending to dress it out on the east bank. Shelf ice complicated our efforts to get it up on the bank. Either a leg, or the head, kept slipping under the ice. We sent Cathy for the Bronco. Once we lifted up on the elk, Cathy was able to tow it up onto the bank. When we opened up the elk, there was no steam, but it smelled fine. Then we dressed out the elk and loaded it into the trailer.

After retrieving the canoe and loading it onto the Bronco, we drove home. On arriving home, we ate those ducks and drank that wine.

Cathy and Ken gave us half of the elk. It tasted fine. Ken said the backstrap on his half tasted really strong, so he fed it to his dog. The rest of their half was fine. I suspect their half was the down side in the ice flow, and the backstrap was soaked in elk blood all night.

Frozen Elk

Early one November afternoon, during the late 1990s hunting season, I received a phone call from Dan Pence. (Dan retired at the same time I did, in 1994, from the Forest Service.)

Dan had received a request from Game Warden Mike Mehn to retrieve a spike bull elk that had been accidently shot the previous day in the Middle Fork of Little Sheep Creek. The area is southwest of Lima, Montana. Dan asked me to go along to help retrieve the elk.

The report was that a member of a hunting party did not see a spike bull standing in the shadows behind a cow elk. When the hunter shot the cow, the bullet went through the cow, killing both the cow and the bull. The hunting party dressed out the spike elk before the hunter turned himself in. Mike contacted a local outfitter to see if he would pack out the mistakenly shot elk. The outfitter was too tied up with his clients to retrieve the elk.

Dan and I unloaded his two horses at the trailhead and rode the first two miles up the Middle Fork Trail. The temperature was in the single digits, and the deeply shaded trail got icier as we progressed. The trail became so icy that we dismounted and led the horses for the last mile to the kill site.

We had to quarter up a thoroughly frozen elk. Dan recalls: "The hunters had dragged the still warm elk carcass onto the frozen creek, apparently to help it cool out, not a necessary precaution in the too cold canyon. The elk's body had melted down through the ice and it froze into place as the body cooled. So, we encountered an elk carcass that was both frozen solid and embedded in the frozen creek. Our first challenge involved rocking the frozen animal back and forth until we got it free of the ice, an effort that took almost an hour. We left a good share of the elk's hair frozen to the ice when we finally got him extracted."

The elk cavity was not entirely cleaned out, and the trachea and esophagus had not been removed. Dan's saw was old, and the blade came apart. Luckily, I had my large Wyoming Game Saw. It took a lot of effort in very cold temperature to finish dressing out the elk and quarter it up. There was no exit bullet wound in the bull, which appeared to verify the hunter's story.

We finally got the elk quarters loaded onto the horses, and led them back to the trailhead, arriving very late in the afternoon. (The elk would go to the local food bank.)

Choices

About ten years ago I had an antlerless moose permit for the South Big Hole. In mid-November, I spotted a large cow moose with a calf by her side. Neither one was aware of my presence, so I had time to determine which one I would shoot.

As I sat there impressed by the size of the cow moose, the following thoughts crossed my mind: The definition of eternity is a bachelor and cow moose to eat. If I shot the cow, I doubt if the calf would survive the winter, given the wolves and other predators in the area. I would have essentially killed two moose. If the cow was pregnant, I could possibly cause the demise of three moose. If the cow was pregnant with twins, then I could be the cause of reducing the moose population by four!

I shot the calf. Hopefully I made the right choice and let the cow produce more calves. With help, and a sheet of plywood, we slid the whole dressed out calf into the back of my Subaru Outback. I drove home feeling I did the right thing for the moose population.

Duck Hunt

Late one fall, in the 1980s, after the general hunting season, I invited Arlan Kohl, a Forest Service engineering technician, to go duck hunting on a Sunday on the Beaverhead River, Montana. It would be about a four-hour float. The temperature was in the teens.

We dropped my canoe off at the Beaverhead Rock launch point and drove down to our planned takeout at the Giem Lane river crossing, just south of Twin Bridges. We left my Bronco with the canoe rack there and drove back to Beaverhead Rock in Arlan's VW bug.

When we returned to the Beaverhead Rock, we noticed a pickup with Butte license plates had arrived and parked there while we were gone. It appeared to us that duck hunters had launched ahead of us.

We went ahead and launched our canoe. Arlan was in the bow to do the shooting. It wasn't long before we came upon two duck hunters from Butte in the slower John boat. We went around them and continued to hunt. This no doubt upset the Butte hunters because we had the good shooting ahead of them. After a while I told Arlan it was my turn to do some shooting from the bow. This was Arlan's first time in a canoe. We hadn't gone too far when he put us crosswise to a fence, and we swamped. My shotgun and my pack containing my shotgun shells went to the bottom of the river. Arlan was able to hang on to his double-barreled shotgun.

After some wading back and forth, I was able to retrieve my shotgun lying in the shallow part of the river. The pack was a loss. We went to the shore to wring out our clothing. I was dressed in a wool "union suit," wool Malone trousers, a wool shirt, a wool jacket, and a wool Scotch cap. Arlan was dressed in cotton thermal knit underwear, blue jean trousers, a wool shirt, a soaked down vest, a cotton Levi jacket, and a cotton ball cap. Here was a candidate for hypothermia!

I told Arlan to get in the bow, that the best hunting was the last hour ahead of us. As we approached a bend in the river, I could see dozens of duck heads ahead of us. I told Arlan: "There they are!"

He was shivering so bad, that when he stuck his finger in the trigger guard, a barrel discharged straight up into the air. A cloud of ducks jumped up and flew off! Arlan never got a duck.

We finally arrived at our takeout, loaded the canoe, and drove back to Beaverhead Rock. Upon our arrival, we noticed that the truck from Butte was gone. I asked Arlan if he was going to make it. He shook his head yes, got out of the Bronco, and walked to his VW. I left as he was getting into his car.

I saw Arlan Monday morning and asked him how it went. He told me that the Butte hunters had removed the rotor out of the VW distributor. He had to hitch hike into Dillon, get a replacement rotor, and hitch a ride back to Beaverhead Rock.

He said he came home and sat in a hot tub of water for an hour. He told me he that he swore he would NEVER get into one of those damn "Indian boats" again!

Persia

For several years after retiring from the Forest Service in 1994, I worked in Dillon, Montana, for local Montana Fish, Wildlife and Parks (MFWP) big game biologist Gary Hammond. This was just prior to the opening of the general hunting season. My job was to man the phone in Gary's office, and answer questions from hunters about regulations and where to hunt

One day I received a call from a gentleman with a foreign accent. He was from California and had never hunted elk. He wanted some recommendations as to where to hunt.

I suggested he "book" with a local outfitter who would pack him in to a "drop camp" in the head of Little Sheep Creek, south of Lima, Montana. The packer would return on an agreed to date to pack him and his elk (hopefully) out.

I informed him that on opening day elk would be chased from Sawmill Creek and pour into Little Sheep Creek through a saddle east of and above his camp.

At the end of our conversation, I asked the gentleman his country of origin. There was a long pause, and he said "Persia." I replied "Oh, Iran! We have a surgeon from Iran here in Dillon, and we love that man." That "broke the ice." The Californian's name was Mike Hannafi, and he was a civil engineer who had immigrated from Iran after the Shah was deposed. He thanked me for the information and said he would like to meet me. I told him I would be working Block Management on a ranch in Horse Prairie. On his way into Montana I could meet him around 6:00 p.m. for dinner in Yesterday's Cafe in Dell.

On the agreed to date, I waited for over a half hour in Yesterday's Cafe for Mike. He didn't show, so I ordered and ate dinner. Shortly after 7:00 p.m. I was walking to my car and met Mike walking to the cafe. He was an hour late because he had not taken into account the time change.

I walked back to the cafe with Mike and had a cup of coffee while he ordered and ate dinner. After dinner Mike asked me to walk back to his car, as he wanted to show me something.

When we got to Mike's car, he retrieved a beautiful Browning hunting knife. He wanted to present it to me as a gift for being so nice to him. I told him I could not accept the gift because I was still employed by MFWP. I gave him the hunting information in the performance of my duty. The gift would be viewed as a gratuity.

Mike was offended. He said that in his culture gifts were given to those who had given a favor. He insisted, so to calm him down I said he could send it to me as a Christmas gift. I would not be employed by MFWP then. This seemed to satisfy him.

I received the knife just before Christmas and gave it to a teen-aged son of a single mom.

Later Mike sent me photos of his hunt. The evening before opening day, he had taken a photo of a dozen elk grazing on the slope on his side of the saddle, just above his camp. He also included a photo of a five-point bull he shot thirty minutes after the opening of the season. Both photos are on my dining room bulletin board.

fall route
o • • •x

1590 – PUBLIC ASSISTANCE (Rescue)
Hank Williams, Jr., 8/9/75
Ajax Lake, Beaverhead N.F.

Hank Williams, Jr., rescue.
Photo courtesy Fred Bridonstine

Chapter Nine

RESCUE

DURING THE PERIOD 1965-1985, while employed by the USFS in Dillon, Montana, I served as a volunteer on the local ambulance, in Search & Rescue, and on the National Ski Patrol.

Saving Hank

Around 3 p.m., on August 9, 1975, I received a telephone call at home from the Wisdom Ranger District. The District informed me that a man had fallen and was badly injured above Ajax Lake. Ajax lake is located west of Jackson, right against the Continental Divide. The District requested that I initiate a rescue. What followed was a rescue involving three aircraft and a flight to Missoula. We had just six hours of daylight flying left to get this done!

I hastily gathering some basic rescue equipment and raced out to the Dillon Airport. After boarding a Cessna 182, we departed Dillon around 3:30 p.m. and flew to the Wisdom Airport, arriving around 4:00. An hour later a Bell 47 helicopter arrived from Hamilton. The helicopter had a covered rescue stokes litter attached to the right cargo rack.

After loading the equipment onto the helicopter, we flew to Ajax Lake, arriving around 5:30. We landed on a flat bench about 100 yards south of the injured man, Hank Williams, Jr.

Hank, and a friend, Dick Willey, and Dick Willey's son, Walt, had been spotting mountain goats above Ajax Lake when Hank slipped on a snow field. Hank landed on rocks below, sustaining severe facial and head injuries, but was conscious.

Dick went for help, leaving Walt with Hank. Dick ran into a Forest Service patrol below Ajax Lake who radioed the Wisdom Ranger District. Then the District got things going. District Ranger Ed Brown was in the area, and on his way to the accident site recruited some campers to assist in the evacuation.

We placed Hank on the scoop stretcher, positioning him on his side so he would not choke on mucous and blood. We carried him to the helicopter and loaded him into the stokes litter.

We flew to the Wisdom airport, arriving around 6:45 p.m. After loading Hank into the Cessna, we departed Wisdom shortly thereafter. Because of the severity of the injuries, I elected to have Hank flown to higher care facilities in Missoula.

We arrived at the Missoula Smokejumper Base around 7:45 p.m. I had Dale Zink, the Forest Dispatcher, radio ahead, and the Base had a Huey helicopter warmed up waiting for our arrival. We transferred Hank into the Huey and flew him to the community hospital.

After delivering Hank to the hospital, I returned to the Smokejumper Base in the Huey. I then boarded the Cessna, and returned to Dillon, arriving around 9:00 p.m.

I sent Hank a copy of the case folder. I never heard back from him. I saw Hank on TV from time to time, after he healed up. He always wore sunglasses, I guess to hide facial scarring.

White Puppy Dog

In 1965, shortly after I was transferred to the Beaverhead National Forest headquarters in Dillon, I was recruited as a volunteer on the local ambulance. Quite often, on my way home after work, I would stop in at Sneed's Sporting Goods store to look at guns and "B.S." about hunting and fishing. Next door to Sneed's was an entrance to a stairwell. Above the entrance to the stairwell was a sign that said: Mint Rooms. Quite often, at the base of the stairwell, lay a large, white Samoyed dog. The dog and I got to be buddies. He would see me coming and jump up to greet me. We'd tussle a little, and then, when I went into Sneed's, the dog would lie back down.

One evening, shortly after I arrived home from work, I received a telephone call from the police dispatcher. The dispatcher said we had an ambulance run. When I inquired as to where to, he replied, "I'll tell you when you get down here"

When I arrived at the dispatcher's office, I was instructed to drive the ambulance down the alley behind the Mint Rooms, climb up the back stairs, pick up a patient who was sick, and deliver him to the hospital. I was advised not to use lights and siren, but just do the job quietly. My attendant was Jim Pribble, a BLM employee.

Jim and I arrived at the base of the back stairwell. I mentioned to Jim that I didn't think we could get the ambulance cot up the steep stairs. Instead, I suggested we use a "chair carry" to bring the patient down the stairs.

I was not aware that the Mint Rooms had been a "house of ill repute." It had been shut down by the city, but the madam was still in business.

When I knocked on the rear door, the door was opened by the madam, wearing thick makeup and reeking of perfume. I heard a loud "woof," and my buddy, the large white dog, jumped up to greet me. Jim turned to me, and with an evil grin said, "Swede, that dog sure knows you.'"

The madam dragged the dog into one of the rooms and slammed the door shut. In another room a 75-year-old sheepherder lay in bed. He was dressed in a union suit with a black kerchief tied around his thin neck. He was diabetic and had consumed a half pint of whiskey. He was a very sick patient.

I sat him up, buttoned up the front of his union suit, and placed his cowboy hat on his head. He wanted a cigarette, so I placed one in his mouth and lit it. He barely had enough strength to smoke it.

We sat him in a chair and proceeded to carry him out. The last thing I heard as we left the Mint Rooms was the dog barking and pawing at the bedroom door. I suspect the dog was wanting to get to his buddy Swede.

That old gentleman died in the hospital that night. But, reflecting on it, at 75 years old, he went out in grand style: "Cigarettes, and whiskey, and wild, wild women."

The next morning, I left the office early to inspect a timber sale on the Wise River Ranger District. The Timber Assistant, Wayne Buckner, and I, broke early to eat lunch. While eating our lunch, I received a call over the truck radio. This radio conversation was going through the Forest repeater, and could be heard all over the Forest, including the Lima, Wisdom, and Madison Ranger Districts. I turned to Wayne and mentioned that it sounded like Wally Gallagher, the Forest Supervisor. It was. I picked up the mike, and said "This is Swede, go ahead." Wally said, "Seen any white puppy dogs lately? Hee, Hee, Hee."

I suspect Jim, my ambulance attendant, couldn't wait to inform our Supervisor's office about the recent ambulance run. For months thereafter, when visiting Districts, I would have to explain what that radio transmission was all about. People would listen with a smile when I would explain that was the first time I ever met the madam.

Trapper in Trouble

On the morning of March 2, 1977, some Search & Rescue personnel, including Marty Malesich, our former mayor, and I, were called out to rescue an injured trapper in Gorge Creek in the East Pioneer Mountains.

Nels Nygren, who owned the Argenta Sawmill, had been running his trap line in Gorge Creek with his son Allen. A culvert under the Gorge Creek road had frozen up, and the water from the creek overflowed onto the road and froze. Nels stepped on the ice. His feet went out from under him, and he fell and broke his hip. Allen, who was only fourteen at the time, built a fire for his Dad, and piled some extra firewood nearby. Then Allen jumped in his Dad's truck and drove to the Jim Marchesseau Ranch in Birch Creek to seek help.

We arrived at the accident site later that morning. The fire was out, Nels having used up the firewood. Nels was beyond shivering, but alive. He lay there wondering how we were going to pick him up with his broken hip.

Just the previous week I purchased the first scoop stretcher in Dillon. Nels was the first patient on it! The lift went smoothly, and we evacuated Nels to the hospital in Dillon, arriving in the early afternoon.

Later local Game Warden Sarge Hoem told me Nels, prior to his accident, had trapped a wolverine around Tendoy Lake in the East Pioneer Mountains. Sarge had purchased the pelt and I saw it hanging on his living room wall.

At a later date, I happened to meet Nels' grandson Jeremia. Jeremia told me that prior to his accident, Nels had set some bobcat traps around Tendoy Lake. When he went to check his traps, he had caught a lynx by one foot. A wolverine heard the ruckus and came down to snack on the lynx. The wolverine also set off a trap, and was caught by one foot, within reach of the lynx. I suspect each critter was blaming the other for its grief and they decided to duke it out right then and there. When Nels arrived, the lynx was dead, and the wolverine was almost dead. The pelts weren't worth much. There was fur all over the snow.

Saving Ken

On June 8, 1977, I received an ambulance request to drive out to the Les Staudenmeyer Ranch to pick a victim of a gunshot wound. (The Staudenmeyer Ranch was about 15 miles north of Dillon, on Highway 41). Keith Reeder and I raced out there in the ambulance.

Two young ranch hands had been "popping gophers" with .22 rifles. When they returned to the bunk house, a rifle accidently discharged. The bullet hit

Emergency Product News Award for Saving Ken. *Left to right:* Dr. Sisk, "Swede" Troedsson, Ken Herrick, and Rick Later

Ken Featherly in the upper right quadrant, exiting out his back. Ken was losing consciousness when we arrived.

We loaded Ken onto the cot. Before we left the bunk house, I alerted the hospital, from the bunk house telephone, that we were coming in with a gunshot wound. I told them that the only thing that was going to save this patient was surgery, so be prepared!

Keith was in the back with Ken. I had my "foot in the fan" doing 85 mph, lights and siren going. Undersheriff Rick Later led the way in a sheriff's department vehicle. When we got to Dillon, I slowed down to 25 mph. As we rounded the corner at the high school, Keith shouted, "He's going into arrest" and started CPR.

When we arrived at the hospital, physicians James Sisk and Dan Eudaily and an ER crew were waiting for us. Dr. Sisk started an IV and was attempting to stabilize Ken while CPR continued. We were informed that the surgeon was out of town, and we'd have to take Ken to Butte.

As I was preparing the ambulance for the trip to Butte, I was thinking, "We'll never make it to Butte in time." Just as we were getting ready to load Ken into the ambulance, in walks Dr. Iddles, the surgeon, and asked what all the excitement was about.

The doctors prepped for surgery. Keith, Rick Later, and I all donated a pint of blood. We all had Ken's blood type!

Doctors Sisk, Iddles, and Eudaily, as well as the great hospital team, saved that lad. The bullet had punctured Ken's diaphragm, front and back, where it bells over the liver, and split the top of his liver. He was in a critical state.

Additional blood, as well as additional medical supplies, were rushed to Dillon from surrounding communities by the Highway Patrol. A respirator had to be borrowed from Anaconda. Members of the community were called in to donate additional blood. Over twenty units were administered to Ken.

Keith, Rick, and I received the Emergency Product News Meritorious Service award for rendering aid that help save Ken's life.

Primate Pills

At approximately 11:00 p.m. on September 9, 1981, I received a telephone call at home from local Sheriff Rick Later. Rick requested my assistance in the rescue of an injured woman who fell off a horse in the East Fork of Blacktail Creek.

Upon arriving in Rick's office, I was introduced to local resident Robert Lewis. Mr. Lewis explained that he was on a horse pack camping trip with friends, in the East Fork of Blacktail Creek The friends, from Olympia, Washington, were a man, Robert Hartz, and his wife, Shelly, a registered nurse. Around 11:00 a.m. that morning, Shelly ducked under a tree leaning across the trail. A limb snagged her sweater. The horse kept going forward, and she was dragged backwards off her horse, falling and injuring her back. After bedding Shelly down in the trail, just south of Honeymoon Park, Mr. Lewis went for help. The husband stayed with his wife.

Rick asked me about the availability of a helicopter. I informed him that I had seen a Jet Ranger land that evening at the KOA Campground, just across the river from me. I called out to the KOA campground around 11:30 p.m. and requested that the pilot return my call. The pilot, Tom Mishler, flying for Hosking Exploration Helicopters, returned my call. I explained the situation to Tom. The plan was to fly Shelly south over the ridge to the Metzel Creek airfield, located on the north side of the Centennial Valley. This would be a short trip. Tom said he would do the flight for free since he was working around Lima Reservoir for an oil survey company. He also informed me that he did not have a litter kit for the helicopter. I told him no problem, we could remove one of the rear doors and load Shelly crosswise on the rear seat. Her feet would be sticking out of the helicopter, but she would be strapped in and safe.

After getting a location of the accident from Mr. Lewis, I called Forest

Engineering Technician Butch Selway, and requested he bring the aerial photo coverage of the accident site to Rick's office so I could examine them for a possible helicopter landing site close to the patient. The examination revealed that there was a large meadow close to Shelly. An ideal helispot!

Rick called in local Search & Rescue personnel Parke Scott, Mike Shaffer, and Chris Kraft to brief them. They were instructed that in the early morning they were to drive to the head of Long Creek, arriving there by 7:00 a.m. From there they would be flown into the accident site to assist in the ground evacuation of Shelly to the helicopter.

Deputy Keith Reeder was instructed to fly in a Cessna 206 and land at the Metzel Creek airfield. After the helicopter had delivered the Search and Rescue personnel to the accident site, the helicopter would pick him up and return to the accident site so he could assist in the evacuation. He was told to instruct the pilot to check up on us if we did not arrive at the airfield in two hours.

We completed our planning around 1:00 a.m. and went home for a few hours of sleep. Around 5:30 a.m., Rick, the pilot, Mr. Lewis, Deputy Reeder, and I, met at Skeet's Cafe for breakfast. After breakfast, around 6:30 a.m., Deputy Reeder left for the airport. The rest of us drove to the KOA campground and flew out around 6:50 a.m.

Around 7:20 a.m. we landed near the accident site, got out of the helicopter, and approached Shelly. The helicopter left to retrieve the rest of the rescue personnel.

Shelly Hartz Rescue

We introduced ourselves to Shelly and explained to her our rescue plans. When I pulled the sleeping bag back to check her vitals, she started to shiver. I turned to Rick and said "Dang, we forgot the Primate Pills." Shelly wanted to know what were Primate Pills. I informed her that if she took two, she would grow fur in two hours. She laughed. For the rest of the trip, she was all smiles.

The Search & Rescue personnel and Keith arrived, and, after loading Shelly onto a scoop stretcher, helped transport and load Shelly into the helicopter. Rick would return to Dillon with the Search & Rescue crew. Mr. & Mrs. Hartz, Keith, and I were flown to the air strip and boarded the Cessna 206. We arrived at the Dillon Airport around 8:40 a.m.

An ambulance met us at the airport, and transported Shelly to the local hospital. There she was diagnosed with a slight compression fracture of the lower spine. She was released shortly thereafter and spent several days at a local ranch until she was well enough to sit in a commercial airplane to fly home from Butte. I sent her a bouquet of flowers with a note that said, "To that beautiful nurse with the devastating smile"

Several days later, Shelly called to thank me prior to leaving Dillon. I suggested she stop by our office on her way out and I would give her some mementos of the Forest. I obtained a container of sugar pills from a local pharmacy and had them labeled "Primate Pills." I placed them along with a Smokey Bear coloring book, a Smokey Bear badge, and a Forest map with the accident site marked on it, into a Woodsy Owl litter bag. Shelly stopped in front of our office on her way out, and I handed her the bag without telling her what was in it.

Later, Shelly wrote me two beautiful letters thanking me and keeping me updated on her recovery. In her last letter she stated, "Your primate pills work wonders for me—no more chilly nights or days for me!—However, there is one problem, that being a financial one . . . my sudden and unquenchable desire for bananas is ruining us . . . oh, dear."

Payback

One of the Beaverhead Ambulance calls I responded to was to a motor-bike accident on the East Bench Road, north of Dillon. Two teen-aged boys had "spun out" on the gravel road and were tossed off their motor bike. They were skinned up but appeared not to be seriously hurt.

My attendant and I loaded them up in the ambulance and transported them to the local hospital to get them checked out. Their Dad, who was an LDS

Bishop, met us at the hospital. The boys were examined and released after their scrapes were cleaned and bandaged.

Sometime later, during the evening, I was called to a local residence. An elderly LDS woman had fallen and injured her hip. After loading her on the cot, my attendant and I proceeded to wheel her out of her home. The LDS Bishop was standing in the doorway. I stopped and asked him if he would have someone walk into my home and sit in my kitchen until I returned. I went on to explain that two of my children were home alone.

My wife was in a Seattle hospital with my oldest son. If this woman had a broken hip, I would have to transport her to Butte. The Bishop said he would take care of it.

Fortunately, the woman did not have a broken hip. After putting the ambulance back in "the barn," I drove back to my home. As I pulled into my back yard, I could see a light in the kitchen window. When I walked into my home, the two LDS boys who I had picked up from the motor bike wreck were sitting quietly at my kitchen table.

You got to respect and admire those LDS folks!

Edmonton

One early spring morning I received a call at my office from the police dispatcher. He said he needed an ambulance driver to transport a gentleman from a local motel to the airport.

Upon arriving at the motel room, I introduced myself to a Canadian couple from Edmonton, Alberta. The previous evening the husband suffered a coronary. After being examined and stabilized at the hospital, he refused to be admitted.

His wife ordered an airplane down from Calgary so he could be flown home.

When I arrived at the airport, there was a twin-engine aircraft waiting to board the patient. I asked the pilot if an attendant came with the aircraft. He said no. I then inquired if the aircraft was pressurized and if he had oxygen for the patient. He said no. I told the pilot that a big snowstorm was forecast and suspected he would file for a flight above 10,000 feet. I asked him what he would tell the "Queen's Men" (Mounties) if when he arrived in Edmonton the patient was deceased.

The pilot got shook. He told me he was never told what he was flying down for. He wanted to know if he could borrow my oxygen. I asked him what guarantee I had I'd get it back. I could see the pilot was perplexed.

I offered to take annual leave and volunteered to attend the patient with oxygen if he could get the wife to commit my air fare back home. She consented and gave me $100 to pay my way home.

Eventually we departed Dillon. Shortly after entering Canadian airspace, the patient complained of chest pains. I asked the pilot to lower the plane's altitude by 2,000 feet. He did. It worked. The patient slept for the remainder of the flight.

When we arrived in Edmonton there was an ambulance waiting. After off-loading the patient into the ambulance, I went into the terminal to book a commercial flight to Great Falls. The ticket agent informed me, with Easter weekend coming up, they were completely booked up. In Canada, Easter weekend is a big deal! I told her I had to be in Dillon the next evening to help teach an EMT course at our local college. She suggested I go down to the next window and try to book a flight to Lethbridge on Time Air, a local commuter flight service serving six cities hourly with Twin Otters.

The ticket agent for Time Air informed they had room for me and my equipment and would be boarding in a half hour. While waiting to board my flight, I looked for the Edmonton location on a huge map of Canada mounted on a terminal wall. I figured Edmonton was way up in Canada and was looking for it in the upper third of the map. It was located in the LOWER one third of the map. Then it hit me how large Canada is!

I boarded the Twin Otter, and on the way to Lethbridge I explained to the gentleman sitting next to me what brought me to Canada. Upon arriving in Lethbridge, I attempted to arrange a charter flight to Montana. I was informed that with the big snowstorm forecast, they were not going anywhere. He suggested I try a bus. There was no bus until morning, too late to make my teaching commitment.

The gentleman who sat next to me on the plane could see I was perplexed. He invited me home for dinner and offered to drive me to the Sweetgrass border station after dinner.

Upon arriving at Sweetgrass, Bernie Jones, brother to Tom Jones, our local insurance agent, walked out of the customs shack. They had both worked on the Madison Ranger District when I was stationed there. I explained my situation to Bernie, and he said not to worry, he'd get me a ride.

After a ten-minute wait, a motor home with three Canadians heading for Disney Land arrived. They would be coming right through Dillon! They agreed to let me on board if I would drive so they could party and sleep.

I drove all night in a howling snowstorm and was back at my desk for the start of my workday. Monida Pass was blown shut, so I let the Canadians park in my back yard and hook up to my power. Monida Pass was opened by late that afternoon.

After filling the oxygen cylinders, I still had $35.00 left over. I sent it to the wife in Edmonton. She mailed it back to me as a donation, which I gave to our local ski patrol.

Sometime later I got an inquiry from the wife. Her husband had passed away and she was still trying to settle with the Canadian government for her husband's plane fare and needed to know the name of the charter flight service. I informed her it was Caribou Aviation in Calgary. That's the last I heard from her.

Odontoid Process

For a few years, while on the Bridger Bowl Ski Patrol, I would take a week of annual leave from my job with the Forest Service in Dillon and patrol the Junior National Ski Meet in Bozeman. Ski racers from all over the country would participate.

The last year I worked the race, the ski hill was "boiler plate" hard. There was one bump in the course, below the midway lift station, that was wiping out many of the racers. The ski coaches from back east thought the course was great. The coaches from the west hated it and were trying to get the course changed.

One morning I was riding up the ski lift and observed a group of skiers gathered around a fallen racer below the treacherous bump. I got off the lift at midway, grabbed an akia rescue toboggan and proceeded down to the fallen racer. (The akia was a surplus military fiberglass toboggan, with attached canvas covers. It was retrofitted with handles, rear aluminum fins to prevent side slipping, and a thick rope rough lock or brake). Inside the akia was blankets, splints, and other first-aid equipment.

When I arrived at the scene, I found out the racer was from Anchorage, Alaska. He told me that when he shot off the bump, he rotated over onto his back, and his back and head slammed on to the hard pack. I performed a quick patient exam. He felt that the main source of his pain was from a shoulder he had injured in a practice run in Anchorage. When he informed me he had tingling in his fingers, that set off alarm bells. I thought "Oh, Oh, cervical spine."

I left the racer's helmet on, and carefully immobilized him in the akia with blankets wedged all around. I sent another patrolman to the bottom of the hill to arrange for a station wagon. I felt time was of the essence because his condition could deteriorate any time.

Choosing the smoothest route, I carefully transported him down the hill. The race physician met me at the bottom and asked what I thought we had. I told him "C-spine" and pointed to a station wagon backing up to the patrol room. I proposed to the physician not to wait for an ambulance from Bozeman, but to remove the akia handles and slide the whole works into the station wagon.

I thought it best to accompany the racer to the hospital in Bozeman. The physician agreed, and we loaded the racer into the station wagon and proceeded slowly into Bozeman.

At the hospital ER the ER physician and I discussed the circumstances surrounding the accident and the symptoms I had observed. I also suggested that they might try to x-ray the patient's spine through the fiber glass akia before they removed him from the akia.

By the time I returned to the ski hill the racecourse had been changed. The next weekend our patrol medical advisor informed me that the racer had a fractured odontoid process. (The odontoid process sits on top of the cervical spine and is the "peg" that the skull swivels on. If it picks the brain stem, it's "lights out") The attending surgeon told our medical advisor that he had been presented with three patients with a fractured odontoid process, and this was the only one to have survived.

I suspect I may have saved that boy's quality of life that day. He had to spend six weeks in a Stryker frame in Bozeman. Attempts were made to transfer him to Anchorage. But after measuring the doors on a Boeing 727, it was determined that the Stryker frame would not fit.

Hang Gliders

From about the mid-1970s through the 1980s, we were using the Dillon Flying Service's Cessna 206 to transport patients from Dillon to higher care facilities in Missoula, Great Falls, and Salt Lake City. Ground transport to Missoula ate up eight hours of our time, when you factor in driving (340 miles round trip), time spent in the receiving ER, refueling, and a stop at a cafe to get a bite to eat. Transport by air took only three hours.

One of our trips to Missoula was to transport a migrant worker with a broken back. He had been helping hang a gate on the Briggs Ranch in Dell, when the gate fell over on him. He had been brought into Barrett Hospital by the Lima ambulance.

The trip was uneventful until we approached Hell Gate Canyon, just east of the Missoula Airport. Andre Morris, our pilot, asked me to look out the plane window. Ahead of us were two hang gliders. We passed BETWEEN both hang gliders! Only about 100 feet separated us from each of the hang gliders! I wonder if they felt our wake turbulence.

The hang gliders had launched from Mt. Sentinel, a popular launching area for hang gliders because of the great updraft when the prevailing wind slams into it from the west.

After we landed, and transferred the patient into a waiting ambulance, Andre went up into the FAA control tower and filed an incident report.

Andre told me that this was not the first complaint about the hang gliders from private and commercial pilots. Our approach through Hell Gate canyon was on a major airway route for aircraft approaching Missoula from the east.

Andre later told me that the FAA had a serious discussion with the hang glider club.

River Rescue

Several years ago, I struck up a conversation with a woman in the Safeway store. During the course of our conversation, she asked me if I had known Leo Cervelli. I replied that I had, and, in fact, I informed her that I had rescued his daughter out of the Beaverhead River. The woman, Meagan Cervelli, exclaimed "That was my Mom!"

In the afternoon of July 14, 1984, I heard on my CB radio that some women were hung up on a "sweeper" (a treetop in the river) in the Beaverhead River, just below the Selway Bridge. Kathy Martinez, and her sister-in-law Linda Cervelli, had launched their plastic raft below the bridge. A short way down, near the Richard Hilton residence, they got swept under the sweeper. The raft was stuck under the sweeper and demolished. Kathy was dragged clear under the sweeper, but somehow managed to claw her way back and perch on top of the sweeper. Linda and Kathy sat on the sweeper for over three hours awaiting rescue. Luckily, Linda had a whistle, which eventually got the attention of someone on the shore.

After hearing the police dispatcher trying to round up Search & Rescue personnel on the radio, I asked my son, Eric, to help me load a canoe on top of my Bronco. We then drove down to the Selway Bridge, located just below town.

We launched the canoe and paddled down to the women on the sweeper. The river was really swift, and the women were terrified. I had them crawl over me to get into the canoe, telling them to sit on the bottom to stabilize the canoe.

We then proceeded to paddle to the shore and left them there in the company of Leo.

The weekend following my conversation with Meagan in Safeway, I was invited to a Mother's Day Cervelli family BBQ, where I was reunited with Linda and Kathy.

Failure to Yield

In mid-April 2020, I bumped into Adrian Stokes in the Safeway checkout line. In mid-September 1972, Adrian was part of a Union Pacific Railroad maintenance crew that was involved in a collision when a "highrail" (a Jeep Wagoneer on railroad wheels) slammed into their motorcar (commonly called a "speeder"). I, and another EMT, responded to the ambulance request and helped rescue Adrian and two of his crew. Adrian recalled the accident, "like it happened yesterday." (He is the only one of the crew who is alive today.)

The accident happened on a rainy afternoon, on tracks just east of the High Bridge, about one mile north of Clark Canyon Reservoir. According to Adrian, it was later determined that the high rail, carrying three railroad executives from Pocatello, Idaho, was doing about seventy miles per hour when it came around a bend and slammed into the motor car. The foreman, Marion Hungate, had time to jump out of the motorcar before it was impacted by the high rail.

The other three men in the motor car were trapped inside by side covers that had been installed to keep the rain out. The motor car burst into flames as it was driven backwards.

None of the executives were injured. The maintenance men were dressed in heavy insulated coveralls, which I cut in order to make patient exams. I determined Stan Smith had a shattered forearm. Bill Wallace was paralyzed from the waist down. Adrian told me he had burns of the face, head, and left arm. He also had a fractured pelvis, a shattered leg, and fractured vertebrae in his neck and back. The foreman was limping around on a sprained ankle.

After administering first aid, we enlisted the help of Montana Highway Patrolman Lorn Anderson, and the executives, to carry the three badly injured men for over ½ mile to the ambulance. We had to stack two of the injured in the back of the ambulance.

When we arrived at Barrett Hospital, Dr. Seidensticker took one look into the back of the ambulance and instructed us to just keep driving to St James Hospital in Butte.

When we got to just north of Feeley Hill, a valve lifter in the engine came loose. Adrian, in the patient compartment, told me he heard the racket, and thought "Good Lord, what else can go wrong?" We clanked the last 15 miles to St James hospital.

After delivering the patients to the hospital, we had the engine checked by a local mechanic. He said we could make it back to Dillon. So, we clanked our way back to Dillon.

Perfect Timing

In 1972, I was employed by the Forest Service. On weekends I volunteered as a ski patrolman on the Maverick Mountain Ski Area. One weekend I rescued a twelve-year-old girl with a badly fractured lower leg. She was in great pain, crying, shivering, and scared. I carefully splinted her leg, and gently bedded her down in the rescue toboggan. The trip down the ski hill was as smooth as I could make it.

It turned out the girl was Kathy France (now DeRuwe), the daughter of the famous Johnny France. (Johnny later became the Madison County Sheriff. He went on to ambush and arrest the "mountain men," who had captured Kari Swenson, a cross-country ski racer who was training for the Olympics. They also shot and killed her friend who was trying to rescue her.)

About six years later I was making a trip to the West Fork of the Madison to inspect a timber sale.

On my way down to the Madison, I stopped at the Ennis Cafe to purchase some chewing gum. Upon entering the cafe, I approached a gorgeous waitress busy at the cash register and asked to buy a pack of chewing gum. She looked up at me, and much to my amazement, came around from behind the counter, threw her arms around me and said, "Swede, how great to see you!" The waitress was Kathy France!

In developing this story, in 2020, I called the France home to inquire as to what year Kathy fractured her leg. Sue France (Kathy's Mother) answered the phone and informed me that Kathy was standing right beside her in the room. Kathy and I had a great discussion. She had retired as a schoolteacher in Oregon and just happened to be visiting her parents. What follows is an email that Kathy sent me later that evening:

> "What a wonderful surprise I had tonight. As soon as I heard my mom say the name "Swede" I leaned in closer to her. I knew it couldn't possibly be my Swede on the other end of the call.

There is perfect timing in everything and tonight revealed that once again. Sure enough, the clear voice and easy laugh proved to be my handsome mountain rescuer from over 45 years ago. Swede, it is an honor that you even remembered me, although I'm sure being the daughter of my legendary Montana father helped. Johnny France has been my hero for so many years and for so many reasons, yet tonight I was able to travel back in time and reminisce about another hero who years ago rescued me off the steep, cold mountain and brought me flowers to my hospital room the next day. I distinctly remember the doctor saying if the ski patrol hadn't been so gentle, I would have had a severe compound fracture because my leg was broken in three places from my ankle to my knee. Thank you for your kindness and tenderness. (By the way, you also gave me a ski pin which I still have tucked in my jewelry box.)"

Ski Patrol Pin

Chapter Ten

DOGS

Harry

IN JANUARY 2007, while conducting business in the Dillon City Hall, Mayor Marty Malesich introduced me to a black German Wirehaired Pointer. Marty said that the dog's name was Harry. The dog had been abandoned for four days in twenty-below-zero weather at the closed down truck stop at Barrett Station, about 10 miles south of town.

Val Prophet, who lived across the interstate from the truck stop, could hear Harry howling at night, and would leave the dog some food. Attempts to catch the dog were unsuccessful until Tara Remley, the city dog catcher, fed Harry some burger with tranquilizer in it.

Tara had the dog for about a week and claimed she could not determine the owner. Marty talked me into adopting the dog. I immediately took Harry to the Veterinary Hospital of Dillon north of town. Veterinarian Lynn Brown examined the dog and said, although somewhat thin, the dog was in good health, neutered, and about seven months old. Lynn gave him some vaccination shots and installed an identification chip.

That night Harry was stretched out with a full belly in front of my roaring fireplace. The outside temperature was nineteen below zero. Harry NEVER LEFT!

URP

A few years ago, I drove my Toyota Tacoma to the Butte Toyota Dealership to get some warranty work done. I walked into the dealership (a big FANCY place)

Harry

with my dog Harry on a leash. There were two service managers, each behind his own pulpit (for want of a better term). I approached one of them and dropped Harry's leash so I could sign the paperwork. After signing the paperwork, I turned around to pick up Harry's leash. Harry had his nose stuck in the cabinet behind the other service manager. Harry's tail was wagging as he was eating the man's lunch! The man was not very happy, to say the least. I apologized and offered to pay for the lunch. He refused my offer.

I went into the lounge to wait out the service. There I was, eating free popcorn and cookies, drinking free coffee, and watching TV. There was a little old lady shuffling around tending to the coffee bar and other maintenance needs. She came over to my chair and said "Oh, oh!" Harry had urped up the service manager's lunch! I was terribly embarrassed, and apologized. She was so sweet about the situation and cleaned it up "like it never even happened."

I went to the service manager and told him he packed a lousy lunch. My dog "urped" it up. The service manager growled that my dog probably got into the hot sauce.

Bonding took a little while. In the evening I would place his dog bed in front of the TV, and he and I would sit there so I could stroke his head and floppy ears.

Harry has been my buddy for over thirteen years. Lynn's good care has helped him live this long. He's become "high maintenance" and struggles to get in and out of a car. I'll keep him until he can no longer stand and walk, and then ask Lynn to put him down.

The trouble with owning a dog is that they don't live long enough.

Trixie

I finally asked my veterinarian to put my dog Harry, down to the final sleep. I had Harry for over thirteen years. Parting was not easy, but it was time.

Ten days later I purchased a six-month-old Border Collie from a breeder in the Missoula area. She was a good-looking dog, but extremely shy, and appeared terrified of me. I suspect it was lacking in human interaction. I had my doubts as to whether I had the patience to get the dog to bond to me.

I began to question my obtaining a dog so young. What was I thinking? I think my grief over loosing Harry clouded my good judgment. I am 86 years old. How long could I give this young dog a "forever home"?

The next day I kept a previously scheduled appointment with my physician. I mentioned to her the loss of my dog, and my acquiring this young dog. My physician mentioned that her sister would go to the local shelter and adopt the oldest dog in the shelter. She would provide a good life for its remaining years. That stuck with me.

That evening, on Facebook, I saw a ten-year-old dog offered for adoption in Stevensville, Montana. The Facebook posting included a photo of the dog.

The dog's original owner had suffered a stroke and was in a rest home. A friend had signed on as an "agent" for the dog and had it for about four and a half months. The dog's name is Trixie. The offer for free adoption was facilitated by the Home to Home shelter network, (home-home.org), a non-profit pet adoption agency. In a phone conversation with the agent, I was informed that Trixie had all her immunizations, was spayed, and was micro chipped. Trixie came with her dog bed, blankets, leash, food, and toys. Trixie is housebroken, friendly and a good traveler in a car. "What a deal!" I thought: "This dog is for me!" I expressed an interest in adopting the dog. The agent stated that the reason she was putting Trixie up for adoption was because her cat did not like the dog, and the dog did not like the cat. She stated emphatically: "The cat comes first!"

The next day I returned the Border Collie and got my money back. The day after I drove to Stevensville and picked up Trixie. All of this occurred in a span of four days.

What a sweet dog! She immediately bonded to me. I couldn't be happier. My "geriatric" dog and I will grow older together.

Trixie

Chapter Eleven

CATS

Cat's Ass

ABOUT TEN YEARS ago a couple that had three cats lived across the alley from me. The husband was famous for his charcoal broiled turkeys.

One Saturday they were hosting a dinner party, and I was invited. The guests included some of the town social elite, and college faculty. The centerpiece of the dinner party was one of those famous charcoal broiled turkeys.

All day, through my kitchen window, I could watch the host, from time to time, lift the lid off the Weber broiler and slather the turkey with his secret potion, then replace the lid.

When it came time for dinner, I walked across the alley and entered the rear of the house through the kitchen door. The dining and living rooms were filled with finely dressed guests, snacking on fancy hors d'oeuvres and sipping spendy wine.

There was no one in the kitchen. On the counter was a huge turkey cooling prior to being served. Out of the cavity of the turkey was the hind end of a cat. I motioned to the host to come into the kitchen. When he came into the kitchen, I pointed to the turkey. The host yanked the cat out of the turkey and exclaimed: "Oh my God, what do I do?"

I replied: "Oh, hell, serve it! They'll never know the difference."

The host served it. His guests raved about how good it tasted. The host kept looking at me, hoping I would not make a wise remark (which I'm usually good for). In retrospect, I should have given the host a thumbs up and told him "Nice job, this turkey is the cat's ass!"

Some years later both small animal veterinarians were hosting a pet information session at the local national guard armory. Student members of the local college service club were assisting in the session. The group was headed by a college professor. I related this story to the professor. It turns out this professor was one of the guests at the dinner party!

Bimbo

About twenty years ago I invited two registered nurses to dinner. Becky, a single Mom, came with her three children and her "significant other," Dean. Becky was a fastidiously clean mother. (I believe you could have done a "white glove" inspection of her home and not come up with any dust.)

At that time, I had a cat I had named Bimbo.

At my place at the dinner table, I had a clean dinner plate under my loaded dinner plate. After finishing my dinner, Becky, who was engrossed in a conversation with her children, did not notice me slip the clean plate out from under my dinner plate, and place it on the floor on the right-hand side of my chair. I did this with a wink to Dean, who was watching this. I suspect Dean guessed I was up to no good. I then placed my empty dinner plate on the floor next to the left side of my chair and called Bimbo over to lick the plate.

When Bimbo finished licking the dinner plate, I looked down and said: "Good job, Bimbo." I then picked up the clean plate from the right side of my chair and showed it to Becky.

I said: "Becky, doesn't Bimbo do a good job? No need in washing this one." and placed it in my cupboard.

Then Becky's vision became glued to her dinner plate. Dean and I burst out laughing. When I showed Becky the plate that Bimbo had licked, she realized the joke was on her!

Chapter Twelve

OTHER STORIES

Grapefruit

In 1952-1953, while attending Louisiana State University in Baton Rouge, I took a part time job as a waiter in an off-campus cafe named The Baker Cafe.

My wages were 40 cents an hour, plus free meals. On weekdays I worked the evening dinner shift, and full day shifts on weekends.

One of the students working the breakfast shift was an easy-going southern boy named Jim (I forget his last name). Jim was a HUGE man who "rough necked" on oil rigs on the Gulf during the summer.

Because the university offered curriculums in petroleum and sugar engineering, the university was attended by quite a few students from South America. Among students who came to breakfast every morning was a student from Caracas, Venezuela. You could tell he came from a wealthy family. He drove a new Chevrolet convertible, flashed lots of spending money, and treated waiters as if they were his servants at home. Every morning he would order a grapefruit with his breakfast. He insisted it be sectioned, so big Jim would oblige with a smile and section it.

One Saturday morning I came into the cafe for breakfast. The university was hosting a state high school basketball tournament. The cafe was full of high school students. The place was bedlam. Jim was moving as fast as a big old southern boy could move.

In saunters the Venezuelan who orders breakfast with a grapefruit. In his haste, Jim forgot to section the grapefruit.

Above the din, you could hear the Venezuelan shout, "HEY GRINGO."

The place went dead silent. The Venezuelan pointed to his grapefruit and demanded it be sectioned.

Jim's face went red. He walked over to the Venezuelan, picked up the grapefruit, and smashed his huge fist into it. Pits and juice squirted up. He set the smashed grapefruit down in front of the Venezuelan and said, "Eat this, you S.O.B."

The boss was watching all of this with a big grin. The survival instinct overcame the Venezuelan, and he commenced to spoon up what was left of the grapefruit.

Nine-Toe Jimmy

The following story was related to me by Jimmy Harrison. Jimmy currently owns the Double H Custom Hat Co., in Darby, Montana. At the time of this incident Jimmy was a member of our ski patrol on Maverick Mountain. This story is submitted with his permission.

In 1970, Jimmy was cutting poles on a ranch near Wisdom, Montana, when he sunk an axe into his boot. Jimmy could feel his foot getting wet inside of his boot. He pulled the boot off, then as he pulled the bloody sock off, a toe fell out. Hoping he could get the toe reattached, he placed the toe into a "snoose" can.

On his way to the ranch house, Jimmy got the desire for a chew as he was crossing a creek. The bloody toe was stuck to the inside of the lid, and when he opened the can, the toe fell into the creek. Jimmy lost the toe.

As the rancher was driving Jimmy to the hospital in Dillon, he asked Jimmy if he had a chew. Jimmy handed the rancher the snoose can. The rancher pinched a dip, stuffed into his lower lip, and handed the can back to Jimmy.

It was then that Jimmy told the rancher about the toe having been in the can, and how he lost the toe. The rancher started to gag and stuck his head out the window in anticipation of throwing up. The rest of the trip into town was uneventful.

This is why Jimmy is referred to as "Nine-Toe Jimmy"!

Death Wish

In 2016 I attended a memorial service in Dillon, Montana, for Bill Murphy (MSO-56). When Bill retired from the U.S. Forest Service, he became active in the National Smokejumper Association (NSA) Trails Program and was a strong supporter of NSA.

Several former Smokejumpers who were active in the Trails program came down from Missoula to attend the service. Among them was Roger Savage (MSO-57). Roger had retired as a pilot with a major airline.

Roger told me the following story about Craig Smith (MSO-57):

(Craig had been a college classmate of mine. When Craig had been my roommate, he recruited me into the Smokejumper program. In 2000 Craig died of Parkinson's disease at the early age of 62.)

Craig wanted his ashes scattered over a peak in the Bitterroot Mountains, south of Missoula, Montana that he and Roger climbed when they attended college. Craig and his first wife, Mary, divorced, and Craig remarried. Craig's second wife (widow) asked Roger if he would rent an aircraft and fly her over the peak that Roger and Craig climbed so she could scatter Craig's ashes on the peak.

Roger consented. He rented a plane and as they approached the peak, the widow inquired as to the name of the peak. Without thinking, Roger replied "St. Mary's Peak."

I wonder what crossed the widow's mind when she found out that the peak has the same name as Craig's first wife.

The last time I revised my will I had my attorney include the name of a high mountain lake where I want my ashes scattered. The lake, Lake Geneva, is just next to the Continental Divide, southwest of Jackson, Montana. The lake flows south and down into Hamby Lake. I have visited over 150 lakes on the Beaverhead National Forest. Lake Geneva is my favorite. The view is spectacular, and the lake contains beautiful Yellowstone Cutthroat trout.

When my attorney inquired as to why I selected that lake, I described the spectacular beauty surrounding the lake and that there were mountain goat beds on the north shore. My wish was that my ashes be deposited on the goat beds. I feel there can be no greater honor bestowed on a man than to have a mountain goat take a dump on his ashes.

Zingers

Dr. Ron Loge, who was my physician for over thirty years, is of a strong Norwegian heritage. I claim a strong Swedish heritage. When the opportunity presents, we use the difference in our heritage to launch a friendly jab at one another.

Some years ago, Ron and I were cross-country skiing in the Grasshopper

Shovel and Sardines

Valley. (The Grasshopper Valley is located about 20 miles west of Dillon, Montana.) At the start of our trip, I mentioned to Ron that I had acquired a small scoop shovel. I had modified the shovel so that the handle could be removed, which would allow the shovel blade and handle to be conveniently carried in my backpack. The shovel could be used for avalanche rescue, or for digging a snow cave.

Ron said, "Let's take a look at it" I pulled out the blade. It was painted a pale blue, and had the Swedish flag painted on it. I said to Ron, "You've just been flashed by the Swedish flag." He grinned, and reaching into his pack, pulled out a can of King Oscar sardines, which he used to "zing" me back.

Wallet

In the fall of 1997, I loaded my canoe on my Bronco, and with Perry Backus, headed for the Centennial Valley, Montana. Perry was a staff writer for the Montana *Standard*. I had invited him to do a story on the "Chain of Lakes." These lakes are within the Beaverhead–Deerlodge National Forest, near the Centennial and Madison Valleys divide. Seven lakes (Elk, Hidden, Goose, Otter, Cliff, Wade, and Smith) make up the chain.

We stopped at Ralph's Exxon in Lima to top off our gasoline. I had made dinner reservations at the Elk Lake Resort and walked over to the telephone booth to confirm our reservation. On entering the booth, I noticed a wallet on the shelf just below the telephone.

It contained the owner's driver's license and credit cards. The wallet's owner was Brian Mutch, son of Bob Mutch. I knew Bob (a former Smokejumper). He had retired from the Fire Sciences Lab in Missoula.

After several hasty telephone calls, I was able to connect with Bob at his home in Missoula. Bob informed me that Brian had stopped in Lima on his way to Boise, Idaho. Brian, a wildlife biologist, worked for the Peregrine Foundation in Boise, and was scheduled to depart Boise the next day to participate in a Condor relocation project!

I obtained Brian's address from Bob, and dashed over to the Lima post office, where I mailed the wallet by Express Mail. I was informed Brian would receive it the next day. It worked! Perry and I continued the trip to the Chain of Lakes. We had a great day, topped off by an awesome rack of lamb dinner at the resort.

Perry's article was published Sunday, October 5, 1997, in the Big Sky Life section of the Montana *Standard*. It was beautifully done! It was well worth the dinner I bought him!

Brian Mutch with Falcon Nestling

Coffee

A few years ago, I went out to the Safeway parking lot and noticed a woman's purse in one of the shopping carts.

Shortly after turning the purse in to the Safeway office, a woman entered the store, appearing in distress. I asked her if she was looking for her purse. She nodded yes. I told her it was in the office, and that she owed me a cup of coffee. She thanked me and went into the office to retrieve her purse.

She must have recognized who I was, or found out who I was. A week later I received an envelope in the mail containing a packet of instant coffee!

.45-110

Up until a few years ago, the Bitterroot Black Powder Rifle Club would participate in the annual Bannack Days (Montana) celebration during the third weekend in July.

The Club would set up a shooting range in Hangman's Gulch and allow the public to shoot their Sharps Rifles at a steel buffalo target some 100 yards distant. Some of their rifles would be on display on tables so the public could examine the rifles.

One year as I was examining the rifles, I noticed a short oriental looking gentleman with a large camera, and large round eyeglasses, standing next to me and examining the rifles. I asked him where he was from, and he responded, "Japan."

I then asked him if he had ever fired a rifle, and he responded "No." I then asked him if he would like to fire one of the rifles. His face lit up with a huge toothy grin, and he shook his head yes.

There were three firing stations. Two were rifles chambered for the standard .45-70 cartridge, and one for the LONGER, and more powerful, .45-110 cartridge. The station for the .45-110 was open, so I walked over to the owner of the .45-110, and pointed out the gentleman from Japan, and said he would LOVE to shoot the rifle. The rifle owner said, "Bring him over." As I led the gleeful Japanese gentleman over the shooting station, I offered to take his photo with his camera as he was firing the rifle. He handed me his camera, sat down, and prepared to fire the rifle.

I shot his photo just as he was rocked back from the massive recoil! He stood up, exhibiting a large toothy grin, and rubbing his shoulder. I handed his camera back to him.

Imagine him showing the photo and telling the story when he returned to Japan. I think I made his day!

World Record

A short time ago I was dating a woman in Red Lodge, Montana.

One evening we decided to attend a movie in Red Lodge. While waiting for the movie to start, I mentioned to my date that we had an opportunity to be listed in the Guinness Book of World Records.

When she inquired as to what I meant, I replied that we might be listed as the oldest couple to have necked in the Red Lodge movie theater.

It didn't work.

Connection

In October 2013, I received a telephone call from a woman who identified herself as Marian Spenser, who lived on Vashon Island, Washington. She said her hobby was genealogy.

Towards the end of the phone conversation, Marian asked me if I was aware I had a half-sister that lived on Vashon Island. Her name is Mary Lou Rowher. I was stunned!

About two years earlier she attended a local genealogy seminar, At that seminar she met a woman who was trying to find her birth mother.

Marian took an interest in the woman's story and volunteered to research the location of the woman's birth mother. Marian's genealogy skills persisted for two years and resulted in closure for both Mary Lou and me.

When I was a teenager, my Dad told me that I had a half-sister. He didn't know where she was. For over seventy years the questions kept haunting me. Was she still alive? If she was still alive, where did she live?

Marian gave me Mary Lou's telephone number. I immediately called her, and after a brief conversation, agreed to fly out to Seattle the next week to meet her. I was met at the Seattle airport by Mary Lou, her daughter and son-in-law, and Mary Lou's friend, who would transport us to Vashon Island. Mary Lou and I hit it right off. I spent four days on Vashon Island at Mary Lou's rental. During my stay, her daughter and son-in-law took us to lunch.

During my visit, Mary Lou, Marian (the genealogist), and I took the ferry to Tacoma. There we had an awesome seafood dinner at a fancy seafood restaurant (Anthony's), on my dime. It was a memorable dinner over which we shared our life experiences and how we found each other.

Marian said it was the most challenging and frustrating research she had ever done. By searching birth, marriage, death, military, and census records, ship passenger manifests, old newspapers, genealogy websites, and Google, she was able to slowly track my mother down. Part of the frustration was that my mother used nine different names (some were similar, but slightly different in spelling) when traveling.

My mother was born in Belgium in about 1910 and spent some time in Russia with her mother and stepfather. They fled Russia after the revolution and traveled to China. She met and married her first husband in the Philippines.

Mary Lou was born in Pennsylvania in 1928. Mary Lou was just three years old when her parents divorced. Her Dad was awarded sole custody. (He later remarried, and his new wife helped raise Mary Lou). Mary Lou's birth mother vanished from her life after the divorce.

Mary Lou's birth mother met my Dad in China in 1933, where they were married. She and my Dad returned to New York, where I was born in 1933. In 1937, my Mother took me to Mexico, where she and I lived for over a year. My Dad came to Mexico and took me back to the U.S. My parents lived separately until my Dad retired in Florida with my Mother.

Both died there. Both of their death certificates list me as their son, living in Dillon, Montana. BINGO! Marian was able to find my telephone number in an old Dillon phone directory, and the rest is history. (Mary Lou died of dementia in 2019.)

Later, at my request, Marian submitted a two-page detailed report about her genealogical search to the Beaverhead Headhunters Genealogical Society. It was published in their December 2013 newsletter.

"Swede" and Mary Lou

ABOUT THE AUTHOR

"SWEDE" TROEDSSON WAS born and raised in the East. His early years in the Boy Scouts developed his love of the outdoors. Following high school, his first job with the U.S. Forest Service began his love affair with Montana and the West.

Summer seasonal work with the Forest Service was interrupted by two years service in the U.S. Marine Corps. This service included deployment to Korea after the truce was signed.

Smokejumping while attending Montana State University introduced him to the diversity of the West, and the excitement that comes with challenges presented in the outdoors.

After graduating from college with a degree in Forestry, his employment as a Forester eventually led him to Southwest Montana. The last thirty one years of his career was on the Beaverhead National Forest. His main duties was preparing and administering timber sales. Other duties "as assigned" was coordinating ground travel restrictions among eight public land management agencies, managing aviation resources, and being dispatched to fight wild land fires.

His volunteer work on the National Ski Patrol would lead him into volunteer emergency medical services (EMS), teaching Emergency Medical Technicians, participating in volunteer ambulance work, and back country rescue. His certification as a private pilot, and managing aviation resources in the Forest Service, enhanced his skills in EMS and back country rescue.

His love of hunting, fishing, canoeing, camping, and volunteer work with Montana game wardens led him into other adventures.

Besides his volunteer work, he found time to help his wife raise three children, introduce them to the outdoor recreational opportunities, and send them off to college. Following his retirement from the Forest Service, he was recruited by Montana Western to teach a course in Map, Compass, and GPS. It would be a satisfying seventeen-year experience.

He continues to reside in Dillon, Montana.